HOW TO OVERCOME POSTPARTUM

From God to My Heart to Yours!

FLORENCE CHUKWU

ISBN paperback: 979-8-9943566-0-9

ISBN hardcover: 979-8-9943566-1-6

ISBN eBook: ISBN: 979-8-9943566-2-3

https://establishwithgrace.com

Printed in the United States of America

Contents

Acknowledgments

I feel convicted to honor those whom God used and continues to use to help us become what He wants us to be for His glory.

To my heavenly Father, Creator, first love, strength, peace, joy, deliverer—my everything! Thank You abundantly for choosing me among so many talented individuals, undeserving as I am, to help bring light to an issue that has long been ignored and has destroyed several marriages, as well as the lives of so many women. Father, to You be the glory forever and ever, throughout all eternity.

Thank You, Father, for giving Your Son to save and free humanity. Without Him, we would still be in bondage. Thank You, Father, for the Holy Spirit, our best friend and guide, who inspired me to write this book. Thank You, Father, for allowing me to write these pages and for inspiring Your children to buy and read this book. I pray that You touch their hearts and speak to them. In the mighty name of our Lord and Savior, Jesus Christ. I am all Yours. Amen!

My loving husband, thank you for supporting me throughout the years and for believing in the mission God sent me here to fulfill. You have been, and continue to be, a blessing in my life and in our daughter's life. You are a big part of this book. I thank God for blessing me with a husband who is loving, calming, funny, and creative. You bring God's joy into my life in so many ways. I love you, my MC baby.

To my hardworking father, Daddy Romaine Muya, and my wise

mother, Henriette Muyunga, I love you both unconditionally. My love for you does not focus on imperfections. I love you simply because God chose you as the instruments to bring my brothers and me into this world. Thank you for everything you are and for all you have done in our lives. I remember growing up and watching you sacrifice your time, your energy, and the little money you barely had to invest in our education and well-being.

Mom, I remember how you would give whatever little money you had to make sure my hair was done. You are one of the reasons I am so dedicated to Jesus. Dad, I remember how you would borrow money so we could have food on the table and go to school, and how you always found a way to make us laugh. I love you forever and ever. My prayer to God is that He honors you with every desire of your hearts, above and beyond anything you could imagine. You are my blessing from God. *Je vous aime tant.*

I am deeply grateful to God for our spiritual father, Apostle Yvan Castanou, and our spiritual mother, Modestine Castanou. Thank you for your love, your obedience to God, and for the powerful example you are to us, your children. I truly believe I would not be where I am today if Impact Christian Center had not been birthed. For that, I am forever grateful.

Thank you, Father Tony, for your love and guidance in our lives. Your obedience to God and your unwavering love are part of the reason we are here today, writing this book. I am forever grateful to you. You are such a blessing to my husband and me. I pray God's blessing over your life. May His grace rest upon you and your family. In the mighty name of Jesus. Amen.

Important Note on Safety and Seeking Help

If you ever find yourself in a situation where your spouse is threatening your safety or the safety of your baby, please leave immediately. Your life matters deeply to God, and staying in an abusive relationship, whether verbal, physical, or emotional, is not more important than your well-being. I believe God can restore, but safety must come first. Take your baby and go somewhere safe.

If you reach a point where you feel overwhelmed and have thoughts of harming your baby or yourself, please do not face that alone. Pray, yes, but also reach out for help right away.

If suicidal thoughts come to your mind, remember they do not come from God. Please seek help immediately while continuing to pray, praise, and worship the Lord.

When I was not feeling well, as I shared in my story, I went to the emergency room. I prayed on the way, but I still went, and God worked through that decision. So please be wise and gentle with yourself. Seeking help does not make you weak. It does not make you less of a strong woman. You are incredibly valuable, and your strength comes from the Holy Spirit who lives within you.

This book is not to discourage you from seeking professional help. On the contrary, I strongly believe that you should seek professional support when needed. This book is meant to help you understand that our heavenly Father can and will help you through whatever situation you are facing, especially when you choose to seek Him first.

I wholeheartedly encourage you to consult your primary care doctor and to follow their medical recommendations. I also encourage seeking therapy, ideally with a therapist who aligns with your beliefs. I personally went through marriage counseling, and I continue to receive counseling today from a believer in Jesus Christ.

I suggest you seek a Christian therapist. I believe that Our Father gave us the ability to help one another and the wisdom, intelligence, and understanding required in different aspects of our lives.

"For the Lord grants wisdom! From his mouth come knowledge and understandin*g*" (Proverbs 2:6 NLT).

Our Father is the source of all intelligence. I encourage you to seek Him to help you get through any situation you face daily.

Author's Note

Let Us Introduce Ourselves

Get to Know Florence

Hello, my name is Florence Chukwu. I am a child of our almighty God in heaven, just like you, and a true believer in Jesus Christ. I am deeply passionate about helping my sisters, at every stage of life and all around the world, live peaceful, joyful, loving, free, productive, and purpose-filled lives in Christ. I am a wife and a first-time mother to a beautiful baby girl who is two years old at the time of writing this book.

I moved from the Democratic Republic of Congo in Central Africa to the United States in 2013. I am a Congolese American and a full-time entrepreneur for my heavenly Father because everything I do is for His glory. I am not a professional writer. Quite frankly, I did not enjoy writing in school, and I believed I was not good at it; that is what the world said. But God had a very different view of me. This book does not come from my own strength or ability; it comes from our Father speaking through me. I cannot wait for you to read what He placed in my heart and shared with me.

From God to my heart to yours.

Get to Know Michael

Hello, my name is Michael Chukwu. Like my wife, I am a child of God and a lover of Jesus Christ, committed to continuing my journey toward eternity with Him. In the meantime, I am a husband and a father to a beautiful wife and daughter, both of whom I am deeply grateful to God for blessing me with. I was born and raised in New York City by Nigerian parents of Igbo descent. I attended university in Buffalo, New York, where I also met my wife, and we have been walking this life journey together ever since.

Originally, I was encouraged to pursue a career in medicine, but God led me in a different direction. My heart has always been to be the best provider I can be for my family, as long as the income is legitimate and adequate. I have worked in many industries and consider myself very adaptable.

This book came to life because my wife and I believe that God has much He wants to do through us, and this is simply one of the ways we are choosing to say yes to His calling. Now that you have had a chance to get to know us a little, let us talk about the reason you are here.

From God to my heart to yours.

Let's talk.

Introduction

It is truly an honor that you took the time to choose this book and begin this journey. I do not believe this is by accident. I believe that our heavenly Father led you here for a reason. Whether you are a believer in Jesus Christ or someone who does not yet know Him, you are welcome here. We are all children of God, though each of us must make a personal decision to come home, which begins with giving our lives to Jesus and entering a real relationship with our heavenly Father.

Whatever your reason is for reading this, please know that it is open to everyone. I truly believe that as you read these pages, something beautiful will happen within you, something that will stir your heart, open your mind, and awaken a deeper curiosity to know Jesus Christ. I believe it will gently lead you into a personal relationship with Him. From my own experience, I can say this with confidence: if you sincerely ask Him to reveal Himself to you, He will.

Postpartum is the period after childbirth, and doctors say it lasts six weeks, but it can go on longer than that. The word "postpartum" by itself is not harmful, but it's what is beyond it that is. This book is meant to help you understand that the problem is not you. You are not crazy, and you are not selfish. You carried a miracle inside of you for about nine months, and now, your body and mind are tired. You deserve to be happy during your recovery, and it is possible to have an amazing postpartum journey.

This is the moment to shift your focus away from the one who seeks nothing but to destroy you. He wants to make your postpartum journey miserable and make you hate yourself, your baby, and even your spouse. That enemy is the Devil himself, the king of lies. His mission has always been to steal, kill, and destroy in any way possible. He looks for moments of weakness or times when we are distracted to attack our minds and bodies.

After childbirth, a woman's body and mind are especially vulnerable. Fatigue sets in, emotions are heightened, and without proper self-protection and care for her family, she can be easily overwhelmed. But listen, there is hope. It is possible not to live in depression. Even if a doctor says you are sick, you can be healed and experience peace, no matter how long the journey takes. I know this because I have walked this road myself. Stay with me and read my story.

God's Word reminds us in John 10:10, "The thief comes only in order to steal and kill and destroy. I came that they may have life, and have it in abundance [to the full, till it overflows]" (AMP). Even if the Devil comes, God says in His Word that He (God) came to give you an abundant life.

So yes, sis, it is possible to enjoy your postpartum journey and walk in peace, no matter what you are facing. Read this again: it is possible to have peace in the middle of the storm. As you apply what is shared, I truly believe that your perspective on postpartum will begin to change. By the grace of our almighty Father in heaven, your heart, mind, and emotions can be restored. In Jesus' name.

Chapter 1

You Are Here Because

Before we talk about the reason you are here, I want you to pause for a moment and take a deep breath. If you are holding this book, it is not by accident. You did not stumble here randomly, and you are not weak for needing support. I believe with my whole heart that God led you here because He sees you, He knows what you are carrying, and He cares deeply about every part of your journey.

My Sister, You Are Here Because

You may be reading this because you are mentally, physically, and emotionally exhausted. You may feel alone, as though you will not get through this and that no one truly understands what you are experiencing, not even your husband, family, or friends. Your marriage may be facing challenges. You may feel like you cannot take care of your home, your baby, or even yourself. Perhaps breastfeeding feels overwhelming, or everything feels harder than you expected. You may have sought help and found yourself doing things that go against the Word of God, or you may have turned to people or practices such as witchcraft, new-age crystals, or tarot cards because you reached a breaking point and felt you could not take it anymore. You feel depressed.

Listen, sis, the fact that you are seeking help is not a bad thing. Let me tell you something important: our Father in heaven knows you completely, even more than you realize. He created you, and He gave you the strength to face the hardest seasons of your life, not alone, but with Him.

I understand the feeling of loving your baby deeply while also longing for the life you had before. At the same time, you do not regret giving birth to your precious child and would likely do it all over again. You have cried many tears. You may have felt like a bad mom for wanting something for yourself. You are in pain, physically and mentally. I understand you, and I do not blame you. You have the right to feel what you feel, but you also have the responsibility to rise out of these feelings because you cannot live or thrive while bound by depression, trauma, suicidal thoughts, or low self-esteem.

There is no joy or peace in staying depressed. Depression consumes not only you, but also your relationships with those around you. Listen, sister love, nothing is impossible with our Father. "For with God nothing shall be impossible" (Luke 1:37 KJV). He has given you the ability to overcome every situation you face. You are not alone. I have been there. I have walked this journey. And I am here with you.

My Brother, You Are Here Because

Brother, you may be here because your better half, your wife, asked you to read this, as she is walking through pregnancy or her postpartum journey. Or perhaps you took the initiative to find this book yourself, and if that is the case, I truly give you so much credit. Either way, you are here because you care. You want to understand. You want to support your wife and walk this journey with her in the best way possible. It is easy to feel like you have no help or no one to relate to during this season, but this book is here to give you perspective, understanding, and guidance.

My prayer is that what you read here will help you approach this season with greater compassion, wisdom, and grace, so that you can support your wife, strengthen your marriage, and also take care of yourself. By God's grace, this journey can be a positive and meaningful one for both of you.

From God to my heart to yours, by the inspiration of the Holy Spirit. In Jesus' name. Amen.

Chapter 2

Pregnancy, Birth, and the Weight of Motherhood

Postpartum is not a joke. It will definitely teach you about self-love, self-esteem, and confidence. It will test you, your marriage, and your relationships in so many ways, good and bad. It will lay out who you are. Some women get through it really well by God's grace, but for some of us, it is bad. In my case, it started pretty fast, so here is my story.

Before we got married, I had a fear (which, again, was the Enemy) that I might not, or would never, get pregnant due to my family history, and because I was oppressed and had no peace. Getting married was also a battle. Anyways, to God be the glory always.

Six months after our marriage, believe it or not, I got pregnant. I was in shock. I could not believe that I was pregnant this quickly because I was oppressed and abused by evil spirits. The Enemy was trying everything to destroy me, my destiny, because he knew how faithful I would become to God, and I am.

I had been sick for more than two weeks, while my husband felt completely fine. At the time, we were both told we had the "flu," but in reality, I was pregnant. We had just returned from Nigeria, so I assumed I had caught a virus during our travels and was preparing to take medication. However, the Holy Spirit convicted me not to take it.

Here is the glorious, amazing part: one day, I was sitting on my bed preparing to pray because I was worried. I heard the voice of the Holy Spirit telling me, "You are pregnant." The voice was quiet and calm. Sis, I said to myself, "Nah, it's impossible. I can't be pregnant." I ran to the bathroom and took a pregnancy test, and guess what? I was pregnant. That day, I took several tests because I couldn't believe it. I probably never would have taken a pregnancy test, and God knew it, because the enemies had put fear in my head that I would never get pregnant. My lack of knowledge made me believe his lies.

I am forever grateful to God and to the Holy Spirit because He was there. He is the one who told me about my pregnancy first, so shout out to my best friend.

"But when he, the Spirit of truth, comes, he will guide you into all the truth. He will not speak on his own; he will speak only what he hears, and he will tell you what is yet to come" (John 16:13 NIV).

"These are the things God has revealed to us by his Spirit. The Spirit searches all things, even the deep things of God" (1 Corinthians 2:10 NIV).

If you are waiting on the Lord to bless you with a child or aspiring to become a mother one day, please trust in the Lord. Never lose hope. Don't believe the lies of the Enemy, please. Ask God to strengthen your faith, give you patience to wait, and help you not to believe the lies of the Enemy.

"And God blessed them, and God said unto them, be fruitful, and multiply, and replenish the earth, and subdue it: and have dominion over the fish of the sea, and over the fowl of the air, and over every living thing that moved upon the earth" (Genesis 1:28-31 KJV).

"You will be blessed more than any other people; none of your men or women will be childless, nor will any of your livestock be without young" (Deuteronomy 7:14 NIV).

While I was not yet married or pregnant, I decided to sponsor (monthly donation) a child for his studies through education in Sierra Leone. I believe that by doing so, I was planting a seed, and God remembered me. I was, and still am, praying for women who are aspiring to become mothers, who have desired to get pregnant for months or years, or who scientifically can't bear children. May God's grace and mercy bless them with twins, triplets, or however many they wish to have.

As you read this, if you feel convicted and can do so, bless a child in need through a donation to an orphanage, school, or hospital. By doing so, you are truly giving it to God. The Bible says, "Abba, Father," the Father of the orphan—God will remember you. Also, pray for those women who want to bear children.

"Because you are his sons, God sent the Spirit of his Son into our hearts, the Spirit who calls out, 'Abba, Father'" (Galatians 4:6 NIV).

Before we even started, the Holy Spirit brought to my attention that, at the end of my pregnancy, I was making sure that my foundation was solid through praying, praising, and worshiping God. I was preparing, not only for my delivery but also for my postpartum journey, but it didn't fully click in my mind until the Holy Spirit reminded me.

Many women spend a great deal of time preparing physically for childbirth, doing things like walking or working out so the belly can drop and labor can begin, nesting, bouncing on a ball, watching videos about delivery and babies, and taking courses. However, we often forget about preparing spiritually: strengthening our spirits, minds, and hearts. Let me tell you this: evil spirits do not care about physical preparations.

I am not saying you should not do those things. Trust me; I did all of them. But if I had not prepared spiritually through prayer, praise, and worship, it would have been very difficult for me to trust God during my postpartum season. It would have been hard for me to keep my faith strong because God works through faith. The Bible tells us: "But without faith it is impossible to please Him" (Hebrews 11:6 KJV).

God responds to faith. Scripture also says: "Then touched He their eyes, saying, according to your faith be it unto you. And their eyes were opened" (Matthew 9:29-30 KJV).

Hypnobirthing

Disclaimer: This section is included for historical and educational context only and does not endorse ancient belief systems or spiritual practices outside of biblical truth.

The Holy Spirit brought this to my attention when I was on YouTube and came across a video about hypnobirthing meditation and relaxation. I did not watch it because I felt a strong conviction not to. I had also seen a few movies in the past about hypnosis, and I did not like them. The entire process sounded like witchcraft to me.

Later, the Holy Spirit prompted me to research the root and origin of hypnobirthing. What I discovered shocked me, especially because I see many Christian women participating in it without realizing the spiritual implications.

The Root

The prefix "hypno" traces back to Hypnos, a figure of sleep in Greek tradition whose name literally means sleep. The modern word "hypnosis" was introduced in the 1840s by Scottish physician Dr. James Braid, who initially referred to the phenomenon as neuro-hypnotism, meaning "nervous sleep."

Long before hypnosis was formally named, ancient civilizations practiced altered or trance-like states for healing, guidance, and spiritual insight. In Greek tradition, Hypnos was believed to be the son of Nyx, the goddess of night, and the twin brother of Thanatos, the personification of death. One of Hypnos' sons, Morpheus, was associated with dreams, a connection reflected in the modern name of the drug morphine. These symbolic associations highlight the long-standing human awareness of the mind's ability to enter altered states.

Historically, trance practices existed across many cultures. In ancient Egypt and Greece, people seeking healing visited sleep temples, where prayer, music, chanting, and rituals were used to induce altered states of consciousness. Similar practices existed in ancient Chinese traditions, Hindu scriptures such as the Vedas, and among Indigenous cultures, where shamans entered trances for healing and spiritual purposes.

The transition toward modern hypnosis began in the eighteenth century with the rise of Mesmerism. Franz Mesmer proposed that healing could occur through what he called animal magnetism, using suggestion to guide individuals into trance-like conditions. Although his theories were later challenged, they laid important groundwork. Dr. James Braid eventually reframed these experiences through a medical lens, giving rise to the scientific terminology of hypnotism and hypnosis that is still used today.

Sis, tell me—what is good about this? How could this not be considered witchcraft? By participating in these practices, you are unknowingly opening doors to spiritual entities. You may not see the effects right away, but later you may begin to wonder why your baby behaves a certain way or why your child struggles. Others may say, "It's just a phase," or "It's a learning curve," not realizing the root of the issue. The Bible tells us to discern good and evil, to be wise, and to be careful about what we get involved in: "But strong meat belongeth to them that are of full age, even those who by reason of use have their senses exercised to discern both good and evil" (Hebrews 5:14 KJV).

Why not meditate on the Word of God and declare it? Don't you believe the Holy Spirit can help you? Is the hand of the Lord too short to save? "Behold, the Lord's hand is not shortened, that it cannot save" (Isaiah 59:1 KJV). Don't you believe God can reduce your pain or even remove it completely—if you ask Him? "Ask, and it shall be given you; seek, and ye shall find" (Matthew 7:7-8 KJV).

Sister, praise and worship can transform your delivery experience. What about practicing breathing exercises while playing Scripture audio or praise and worship music in the background and inviting the Holy Spirit to help you?

Do your research before doing anything. Ask the Holy Spirit. Do not participate simply because everyone else is doing it or because it sounds appealing. The cost can affect both you and your baby, not only in the short term, but also in ways that could have been avoided if you had sought God first. If you have already participated in it, it is not too late. Acknowledge it, repent, ask God for mercy over you and your child, re-nounce it, and begin declaring the Word of God. Plead the blood of Jesus. (Be sure to get the *Overcome Postpartum Guide* when it becomes available.) Be a wise woman.

When we found out we were expecting, my mental state was all over the place. I felt surprised and anxious at the same time. I want to highlight that feeling anxious is not from God; however, I was grateful to our Father for His strength.

My pregnancy journey was amazing, long, and tiring, with many ups and downs. Our baby girl was a beauty inside and out, and she still is. She kicked me a lot in my belly! Some-times it was painful, but I somehow enjoyed it. AHAHA! It's crazy what we go through by bearing a child, right? All these kicks—how could I enjoy my baby kicking me so hard that I couldn't even walk? I don't know, sister-love, but I know God gave us, women, the strength to endure such a high level of pain.

My delivery was long, and I ended up having a C-section, which I wasn't planning on. I prayed to our Father for a less painful birth experience, and I received what I was praying for. Believe it or not, I did. I didn't experience pain at all, un-like some sisters. I felt pressure, but I was walking the next day and continued walking even after going home. Yes, I was on medication, but I wasn't in pain. It may sound crazy, but it is the truth. I strongly believe that God answered my prayer.

Our Father might not answer in the way you expect because

He knows what is best for you, in this case, for me. He answers based on what He knows is most beneficial for you and your precious baby because He gifted you this child.

When I went home, I wasn't taking any painkillers. I didn't do it on purpose, okay? I simply kept forgetting to take them. So yes, believe me when I say I didn't experience pain, only a little pressure.

If I had a vaginal birth, it might have been painful, and my recovery might have been longer. So I prayed, trusted, and let God act as He wished because His will is mine and always welcome. I want to mention that while I was in the hospital, I didn't produce enough milk. The result of that was my baby losing weight, from eight pounds to seven pounds. For some, this might not have been as concerning, but as a first-time mom with no experience, I felt terrible. The guilt and the feeling of being a bad mom weighed heavily on my heart. I was sad, upset, and felt defensive. My heart was crying as I looked at my tiny baby, whom I had to take care of, while feeling as if I was already failing.

Not producing enough milk was something I struggled with for a few months. The guilt was unbearable, but by the grace of our Father, He helped me get through it. I strongly believe that He can and will help you as well.

Today, my baby is a toddler, a healthy girl, thriving on formula and now some food. She is fourteen months old at the time I'm writing this, so glory be to our almighty Father.

Sister, don't feel bad if you couldn't produce enough milk; your baby will be healthy regardless, by the grace of God. Your child will grow in strength and wisdom just like Jesus did: "And Jesus grew in wisdom and stature, and in favor with God and man" (Luke 2:52 NIV).

Finally, going home, oh, thank You, Father! I was just over it. Hospital food wasn't as good as homemade food; the bed was small and uncomfortable, and the hospital was cold to protect against bacteria or something. But it was tough having my baby in such a chilly environment, as I didn't want her to catch a cold. As a first-time mom, you know what I'm talking about.

Anyways, I was happy to be home with my baby, my husband, and my mom. Yes, my mother stayed with us for eight weeks to help, since I was a first-time mom. I was grateful to our Father for that.

Chapter 3

When Postpartum Turned Dangerous
The Emergency Room

By Sunday morning, my body wasn't feeling right. I wasn't in pain, just tired, sleepy, and out of breath, like I needed oxygen. I went outside, just in front of the house, to breathe in some fresh air, but still something was off. I ate, but I still didn't feel well. I went out again for fresh air, but nothing changed. This went on from morning until evening, so I told my husband, and he said we should go to the emergency room right away and not even start guessing what was wrong with me.

I heard a voice saying, "Just sleep, and you will be okay." That voice was clear. It was the Devil trying to make me think everything was fine, when things could have gone worse if I had given in to that thought.

I was worried and sad to leave my baby because it had only been two days since we came home. Just so you know, I had gestational diabetes. Thank God, it didn't affect my lovely baby girl. My blood pressure was great during my pregnancy. Oh, our Father was so good, and He is still so good to me!

I thought maybe my sugar was low, but my breathing wasn't right. Before leaving the house, the Devil tried to convince me to sleep again. I heard it clearly in my mind. One of the Enemy's tricks is to make you believe that some of these thoughts are yours or that they are good thoughts, but in reality, it's him. It was like he was speaking to me. He had an agenda for me. It was death. If I had stayed at home, I would have died, because that was the plan. But thank God my husband decided we should go to the hospital, and my mom stayed at home with our baby.

Sister, trust your instincts. Many women die after giving birth because they don't pay attention to their bodies. They don't listen to that small voice telling them to go to the emergency room and get checked. I would rather go to the hospital and let the doctor and nurse tell me there isn't anything wrong than to stay home and let things get worse. Yes, pray to God, which I did, but also go get checked. Isn't it God who gave humans the ability to become doctors, lawyers, and more? Please, sis, be a wise woman.

As we were walking toward the car, I felt sad because I had just given birth and had to leave my baby behind. (I pray for those who leave their premature babies in the hospital. I can imagine how hard that must be. May God give you strength.)

On the way to the hospital, my husband suggested that I call one of the nurses who had taken care of me in the postpartum room. She was so kind and caring that, on the day I was discharged, we took a picture together and exchanged phone numbers. I called her, and she said it could be low blood sugar, stress, or something else, so I should go to the ER. I told her we were already on our way. She suggested that we stop at a gas station and buy some candy or chocolate, as it can help if blood sugar is low. During that whole conversation, I still felt out of breath.

My husband bought the chocolate and gave it to me. I started eating it and let me tell you: I felt a little better. My breathing wasn't as bad. So I believe God was in control of everything and still is. He inspired my husband, through the Holy Spirit, to call the nurse because I wouldn't have remembered.

No matter what you are going through in life, remember that God controls times and seasons. Daniel 2:21 "He changes times and seasons; he deposes kings and raises up others. He gives wisdom to the wise and knowledge to the discerning" (Daniel 2:21 NIV).

At the emergency room, we waited for hours before a nurse finally came to get me. She started taking my blood, checking my vitals and heart, and running exams. I didn't even mention during check-in that my heart was hurting or anything. I don't know why; I can't explain it. The only issue they identified at first was my high blood pressure and swollen feet and body. At that moment, that was all I knew because the nurse told me, and I believed it was just that, nothing more. I was curious and impatient to get my results and go home. But as I said, the Devil was planning something. Fortunately, God was, and is, in control.

While we were waiting, I was praying in my heart, calling my mom so she wouldn't worry, and checking on my three-day-old baby girl. Sis, it wasn't easy sitting there waiting for hours, more than five hours. I want to emphasize that my feet had been swelling throughout my entire pregnancy, making it difficult for me to walk and stand for long periods. I could only walk for about thirty minutes before I started feeling pain in my hips, back, and legs. But as I mentioned, I enjoyed being pregnant, and I would do it again. I also want to emphasize that I was on medication during pregnancy to avoid developing preeclampsia.

A few more hours passed before the doctor informed us, to my surprise, that I had postpartum preeclampsia, which was why my blood pressure was high and not going down. I heard that some women experience severe headaches, itching, and more. At that moment, I was scared. I thought they would give me medication and send me home. Instead, the doctor told the nurse to admit me to a room.

Chapter 4

The Hospital Battle and God's Intervention

I was a little relieved because it was the same emergency hospital where I gave birth, so it felt easier. They already had all my details, and I was in a place I was already a bit used to. Looking back, I was so grateful to God that He made things easier for me, even though I wasn't feeling well. I was weak, and I remembered I had a C-section, so I was feeling a little pressure but no pain, and I was walking, just slowly.

Sis, God will not let you walk alone. He was there with me every step of the way, and I truly believe He will be with you, too.

The Bible says: "Even when I walk through the darkest valley, I will not be afraid, for You are close beside me. Your rod and Your staff protect and comfort me" (Psalm 23:4 NLT).

Thankfully, the same nurse who took care of me when I came to give birth was the one who put me in the room. I believe it was God's way of telling me that He was there with me and that He was in control. When she placed me in a small room, I asked her, "When can I go home?" because I was tired and drained from being back in the hospital. She told me that if my blood pressure didn't go down and the medication wasn't working, they would keep me on potassium for twenty-four hours! Apparently, potassium has side effects that vary for different people.

She left the room, and I told my husband that I wasn't staying for another day. I had already been there for four days, and I wanted to go home and be with my baby. But I'm grateful to my husband for comforting me. I appreciate him for being calm, not panicking, just calm, trusting that God is in control, and reminding me that I needed to be patient so I could get well for our baby.

I decided to start praying, worshiping, and declaring healing over my body with the blood of our Lord Jesus Christ. I was determined to heal and go back home within a few hours. I didn't want to stay. I understood what Jesus did for us on the cross. I knew He had already healed me. This is what the Bible says: "But He was pierced for our transgressions, He was crushed for our iniquities; the punishment that brings us peace was on Him, and by His wounds we are healed" (Isaiah 53:5 NIV).

I had already made up my mind to reject that condition (postpartum preeclampsia) and rebuke it in Jesus' name. I continued with prayer, worship, and declaring the Word of God and healing over my life.

While the nurse was getting ready to give me potassium, I had no doubt about my healing. My faith in God and His Word was strong because I had been miraculously healed from severe headaches before, and I had never been to a doctor for that. From childhood until 2019, I suffered from those headaches. But it was spiritual. Those migraines were so severe that I couldn't even open my eyes or talk. All I could do was stay in a dark room, in silence, and cry without tears.

The situation did not shake my faith. I was simply over it, exhausted, physically and emotionally drained from being in the hospital. Since the beginning of my pregnancy, I had been going in and out so often that it had become too much. If you've ever been pregnant, you know exactly what I mean. The only time I felt truly happy was when I had to go in for an ultrasound. I was never late for that one!

We decided it would be good for my husband to go home and stay with my mom and the baby. As a new parent, I needed him to do that and return to the hospital the next day because I strongly believed God was with me.

The nurse came to start the potassium treatment. She told me that I had to stay in bed with no movement for twenty-four hours. So basically, I couldn't walk, eat, or drink water for that long. The more I moved, the higher my blood pressure went. They put a machine inside my feminine part so I wouldn't pee on myself. God was my strength. I could never have gone through this by myself. It was impossible. God is truly a Father who takes care of His children.

The nurse tried to put in an IV so I could get potassium to treat the preeclampsia, but she couldn't find my vein. She said my body was so swollen that my veins were not visible at all (just imagine the level of swelling I had). She called another nurse, and another, and another, and so on. I saw more than five nurses; I couldn't tell you how many came to put an IV in me. They even called a specialist doctor and nurse in this area, but neither could find my vein. They tried various tools and machines, but still no sign of my vein.

While all of that was happening, I was extremely weak. My arm and hand started to hurt badly because of all the needles poking into my skin. Some of them were big. But I kept praying, "God, help me."

The nurses were worried; I could see it on their faces. Preeclampsia and high blood pressure can lead to many complications and even death. To lower my blood pressure, the preeclampsia had to be treated. According to the doctor, if they hadn't found the vein, things could have quickly gotten worse. There are many articles that talk about postpartum preeclampsia, so I advise you to do more research if you want to learn more.

My physical body was weak, exhausted, and in pain from lying in bed without any major movement. But my mindset and spirit were strong and determined to go home. God's strength and presence were with me. I knew this situation was warfare. It wasn't just physical but spiritual. I knew the Devil was trying to do something, and I had the conviction to get my brothers and sisters from church involved without giving them too many details, just enough to have them intercede in prayer for me. So before my husband went home, I told him to let them know and to start praying for me.

Sis, it's important to make sure that your entourage is filled with people with the same faith as you, people who can pray for you. That's one of the most powerful things you can ask for in situations like this. I was also praying, worshiping, and taking authority against any evil agenda. At some point, my body was so weak and tired that I was just quiet and prayed in my heart. I'm grateful for God's mercy on me and for the lives of my brothers and sisters in Christ—for their support in prayer; it truly helped me in this battle.

I was in and out of sleep, and God really made sure I was somehow getting rest and sleep even though I was so weak and tired. I don't know how. I can't explain it; it was supernatural. While I was asleep, I didn't have any nightmares, and while awake, I didn't see anything evil. I had peace.

One of the nurses who also took care of me in the delivery room came and asked how I was doing. She said she was going to try again to get the needle in. My eyes were not fully open, but I could see her face, and I knew something was about to happen. It was God's intervention because she was just a regular nurse. She took care of me when I came in to give birth (she was so nice and caring). She wasn't a specialist nurse like the others I had seen. I heard her say, "I'm going to try the IV again." My body was still swollen, nothing had changed, no sign of my vein, and I was still praying in my heart.

God will never let you down. He will never let the Devil destroy you if, and only if, you give your life to Jesus, surrender to Him, obey His Word, and trust Him.

The nurse tried just once and was able to get the IV in. The needle went in at the same place the previous doctor and nurse tried, and I was still swollen without seeing the vein. I was happy, rejoicing. WOOOOOW! Glory goes to God. In Jesus' name. It had probably been more than an hour since they were trying to get that IV in, and just one nurse made it look so easy. Isn't He God? Just one IV went in after so many failed attempts. I couldn't even tell you how many, but I knew there were more than five needles poking my skin.

The Devil could fight me as many times as he wanted, but he knew he couldn't fight God's will in my life. Deep down, I knew it was not the time for me to die because I wanted to accomplish God's will. I wanted to do what God sent me on the earth to do, and it was not my time yet. At the same time, I understood that the upcoming year, God would guide me through working for His kingdom. His will is my purpose, the reason why I have a plan that He created for me to follow, so the Devil's attempts constantly failed.

The Bible says in Isaiah 54:17: "No weapon forged against you will prevail, and you will refute every tongue that accuses you. This is the heritage of the servants of the Lord, and this is their vindication from me, declares the Lord" (NIV).

Since God said you were healed through His Son, Jesus Christ, then believe it and declare it out loud in your life.

"He says to her: 'Daughter, your faith has healed you. Go in peace and be freed from your suffering'" (Mark 5:34 NIV).

And in Isaiah 53:5, "By His wounds we are healed" (NIV).

I strongly believe what the Bible says because it is the truth. God speaking to us. No one can tell me otherwise because I am a true testimony that what the Bible says is real. I didn't need a pastor or anyone to convince me. God did it through His Word, and I believe He can do the same thing for you. Seek Him and see for yourself. Don't be too quick to judge or believe what other people say about the Bible or being a follower of Jesus Christ. Make your own judgment by trying; then you can have your own opinion.

I was so grateful to our Father God for His intervention. The nurse told me not to move my arm and ran to call the doctor since she was able to put the IV in. The doctor came and started the potassium to treat the preeclampsia so my high blood pressure would go down, and they put me on medication. Sometimes God uses people to intervene in our healing. So when you feel that something is not right, even if it is a little pain for any reason, go to the emergency room. Don't fool yourself by saying that God will heal you. Yes, He can if that is His will, but if His will is to use people to help you, how would you know? Please, I urge you to act wisely.

From there, I was a little weaker, and my vision was blurry. I didn't experience anything more, but my mind and spirit were strong by the grace of God. I stayed in bed for twenty-four hours.

My husband came the next day with my mom and my precious baby. Oh, I missed her so much and was so happy to see her. I was just in love. She is so beautiful inside and out. I even tried to pump milk and was able to get a little for her. At that point, I was allowed to get some food, and it wasn't that bad. My husband and mom stayed for about an hour.

When they left, the nurse told me that they might keep me for a few more days until my blood pressure went down, which was expected since they started the treatment. I was honestly not happy about it, so I kept praying, worshiping, and declaring the Word of God over me.

The nurse stopped the potassium treatment; the other nurses had to come check my blood pressure every thirty minutes and gave me medication to help because it was still a little high. It just shows you how high my blood pressure was. Another nurse came and checked my blood pressure again, and that happened repeatedly.

I was over it because I had to spend another day at the hospital, and at this point, it was day two. I kept asking the nurse, "Can the doctor tell me when I can go home?" because I felt as if I had been there for a week, and my delivery was also long. I spent four days, so you can imagine how tired I was. Slowly, my blood pressure went down to a level that was reasonable for the doctor to let me go home on the morning of day three.

No one knew besides my mom and a few of my sisters and brothers from church because I didn't want to alarm my family members. My dad didn't know either because of his own health challenges. (I don't know if my mom ended up telling him; I don't think he knows even now. I might be wrong.) I spent a total of two and a half days in the hospital. The doctors prescribed medication to take home.

I was still on a low-dose medication for my blood pressure, which helped stabilize it as it was going down. I knew that I already had the victory, and I was so happy and excited to finally spend time with my beautiful little baby girl and eat good food. After that, I had no more complications, although I was still on medication.

On my next follow-up with my primary doctor, my blood pressure was much better. So, I visited her every three months, and now my blood pressure is back to normal by the grace of God. Sometimes, I check my pressure at home to ensure it is normal.

On my last follow-up, the doctor said my blood pressure was good, and I asked her when I could stop taking my medication. She told me that it had to stay low consistently for her to take me off it, and I had to lose weight. That news didn't make me happy at all, but I know I'm already healed in Jesus' name by His blood, and my blood pressure is back to normal. Now my C-section is completely healed, and I have no pain. My sugar level and my baby's sugar level are also good—all by the grace of God.

You might go through tough times in your pregnancy or postpartum, but you don't have to go through this alone. That peace and assurance are only in our Lord and Savior, Jesus Christ. Our Father in heaven gave His Son for us. Get to know Him for yourself by accepting Him into your life as your Lord and Savior. Romans 8:32 says, "He who did not spare His own Son but gave Him up for us all—how will He not also, along with Him, graciously give us all things?" (NIV).

I did not share this part of my story to frighten or discourage you from getting pregnant. Rather, I want you to know that no matter how hard your pregnancy journey or postpartum may have been, seek God and put your trust in Him. He was with me every step of the way, and I am confident He will be with you. Receive Jesus Christ as your Lord and Savior if you haven't. Give yourself (mind, body, heart, soul) to Him, and your life will never be the same. You will overcome any battle, receive healing, peace, and everything your heart desires, even in the middle of the storm, because our Father loves you. Before your birth, He knew you. It is okay if you feel dirty or have done many bad things. He still loves you. He loves you unconditionally, and nothing can separate you from the love of God.

"Who shall separate us from the love of Christ? Shall trouble or hardship or persecution or famine or nakedness or danger or sword?" (Romans 8:35 NIV).

Chapter 5

What Research Says About Postpartum

Society has predominantly chosen to keep issues related to postpartum experiences silent. Historically, the medical and psychological needs of women following childbirth have frequently been neglected.

One of the leading medical universities, Johns Hopkins, stated in its article that baby blues and postpartum depression are likely to occur. In fact, many new mothers experience baby blues. These hormonal shifts can lead to feelings of anxiety, crying spells, and restlessness, but they typically resolve within the first two weeks after giving birth. Also known as postpartum blues, the baby blues are a mild and temporary form of depression that diminishes as hormone levels stabilize.

Research shows that 85 percent of new mothers suffer from postpartum blues. One moment, you might be joyful, and the next, you might be overwhelmed and in tears. A history of mood or anxiety disorders is also a factor. Postpartum depression is 30 to 35 percent more common in people with bipolar illness, depression, or anxiety. Similarly, women who have experienced signs of depression during past pregnancies are likely to experience them again.

Symptoms of postpartum depression may last for months or even years if treatment is not received. Three years after the birth of their children, 25 percent of participants in one research study were still depressed.[1]

My observation: I have nothing against science. In fact, it is God who gave men the ability to name things, cure diseases, perform surgery, and do many other endeavors. For that, I bless our Lord and Savior Jesus Christ.

I'm not here to say that the research done is false. I know they put a lot of work into these studies, and I respect the scientists. I'm here to help you realize that these are facts—facts that are good and facts that are bad. Either way, facts are facts. However, facts are not always normal, natural, or good for you as a born-again Christian, a believer in Jesus Christ. You should always live by everything that comes out of the mouth of God. Let the truth (the Word of God) become your reality.

Scientists can agree that they can't prove everything; they are limited to what God allows them to know or not know. Even

---

[1] Johns Hopkins Medicine, "Postpartum Mood Disorders: What New Moms Need to Know," accessed January 13, 2026, https://www.hopkinsmedicine.org/health/wellness-and-prevention/postpartum-mood-disorders-what-new-moms-need-to-know

though some of them don't believe in Jesus Christ as Lord and Savior, some believe there is a higher power. Quite frankly, they haven't scientifically proven that they can cure everything.

I'm here to help you rely on the truth from a biblical standpoint. Depression, anxiety, rage, anger, suicidal thoughts, frustration, and so on are not normal; they are spiritual. There is something beyond it... or I would say, someone beyond it: the Enemy. Science cannot prove it, but God has allowed us to know about it for a reason. The reason is so that we may have knowledge through the Word of God and the Holy Spirit who lives in us.

Yes, these feelings will come; we can't disregard them. You might cry, or you might not cry; you might feel upset, or you might not. But the reality is, if those feelings keep coming back and begin doing more harm, then there is something else happening or someone involved: the Enemy. Will you lack sleep? Yes, you will because you have to feed the baby. That is why I encourage you to have a good support system. Reach out for help. When the baby sleeps, get some sleep. Or give the baby to your mom or husband and take two to three hours of rest.

I know you may say you can't sleep because you have to clean bottles, cook, and do other things. But for any reason, sis, please don't stay in a place of complaining or blaming others. Instead, take a moment to praise God for His grace as you carried a child for nine months. Thank Him for the gift of giving birth. Do you know how many women could have been chosen in your place? Sis, please sleep. You will have time to clean or do what you need to do later. You must give yourself grace. It is okay if there are still dishes in the kitchen for one more day, two, or three. Please try to sleep when the baby is sleeping. That is what I did by God's grace, and it helped me a lot. You can even plug in your headphones and listen to Bible audio or worship music while resting to strengthen your spirit.

When my mom was awake, she took care of my daughter while I slept for about two hours. I took breaks and slept here and there because the truth is, your body carried a baby for nine months. Your body changes tremendously, and it is recovering.

Recovery is different for every woman; for some, it takes a couple of months, for others, a year or a year and a half. That was my case. So give yourself grace. Allow your body to re-cover at its own pace by God's grace and pray about it.

The Effects of Social Media

Social media often shows "perfect recovery" mothers, those with strong support systems, back at the gym and smiling. Not all, but some. I'm not saying all of them are lying, but some are. It affects other mothers, especially first-time moms who begin comparing themselves or forming an ideal of what post-partum recovery should look like from a worldly point of view, not a biblical one. Many of us moms, especially first-time moms, focus on physical appearance, which is not wrong. However, the pressure to get back in shape quickly, to look a certain way, or to appear strong, instead of focusing on mental and spiritual recovery from a biblical perspective, is absolutely not recommended.

Sister, your body may not be ready to return to the gym right away. You may still need rest and healing. Instead, focus on your mental health and inner well-being. Do things that make you feel good while allowing your body to rest. For example: get your hair done, take a shower, get your nails done, go for a walk, eat balanced meals, go on a date with your husband, watch sermons together, pray together, laugh together, relax, or have someone you trust watch the baby.

I'm not saying do all of this at once. You still have to care for your baby, so do one or two things each day that bring you joy. If writing makes you happy, then write. If you need to talk, ask God to direct you to a good therapist, but first, make the Holy Spirit your first therapist. Talk to Him. Have a conversation with Him. Trust me; He will speak back to you. If you truly desire a relationship with Him, it will amaze you how real the Holy Spirit is. If you feel led to see a therapist, ask God for direction. If you have a good pastor, reach out with your spouse; don't go alone. If your support system is strong, reach out with your spouse. In everything, pray and ask God for direction. Make Him your confidante. Remember, you are not alone. He is with you.

My sister, what you may not know or realize is that someone has had, and still has, an agenda against you and your precious baby. Now, let me explain how and why you should shift your focus and stop condemning yourself as a bad mother, wife, or woman.

Chapter 6

Guarding Your Mind and Walking in Victory

Doctors say it is normal to have mood swings, less sleep, and anxiety after giving birth because your body changes so much and your hormones are all over the place, not to mention the fear of being a bad mom.

Let me tell you, sis: yes, these emotions can and will come and tempt you to do wrong, but you don't have to stay there and believe them. You don't have to accept having your emotions all over the place. Yes, as women, we are emotional, but it is important to learn to control, or crucify, our emotions, so they don't take over and become an open door to the Enemy. The Bible talks about crucifying our flesh, choosing not to be fearful, having low self-esteem, or believing you are a bad mom or wife.

As I have mentioned before, it is not okay to stay in fear, depression, rage, and moodiness for months and even years. And as we know, it can take more than six weeks. I had my baby girl, so I know what it feels like, but once you choose to have God as your source, He will give you the strength and guidance to overcome.

Have you heard people say that feelings come and go? The question is: how do these feelings come and go just like that? Do we wake up in the morning and want to feel sad and anxious? Do we call anxiety to come into our minds and take control? Is it normal to scream at your newborn baby for crying, even if you had little to no sleep? Ask yourself: why would someone wake up in the morning and feel depressed? Do you want to be depressed and stay that way for months or even for a day? Of course not.

I'm sure many of us have seen videos online of women screaming at their newborns, shaking them hard, saying terrible things, and some even throwing their newborns or killing them. Is that normal? Some call it postpartum rage or depression. Here is what God says: "Get rid of all bitterness, rage and anger, brawling and slander, along with every form of malice" (Ephesians 4:31 NIV).

The Devil knows very well that after giving birth, a woman is naturally tired and weak from labor or a C-section, after carrying a baby for nine months (close to ten). He also knows you will get less sleep at night because you have to wake up to feed your newborn. The Devil will always use a moment of weakness to tempt us mentally. Depression or rage does not come from you, but from him, but God calls us to peace.

"Let the peace of Christ rule in your hearts, since as members of one body you were called to peace" (Colossians 3:15 NIV).

Depression, feeling depressed, can be described as the absence of joy and peace. I'm talking about the internal absence of joy and peace that shows on the outside through loneliness, sadness, and heaviness. Where there is no joy, there is no peace, and where there is no peace, there is an open door for the Devil to come and play with your mind and make you believe you are the problem.

Everything starts with a thought. Most of the time, we let our minds wander without paying attention. A woman can think about so many things in a matter of seconds. Have you noticed that women often multitask, doing several things at once? (See the Proverbs 31 woman.) How can we do something if we haven't thought about it, or been inspired by someone, or, I would even say, an entity? It is simply not possible.

Sometimes, if not most times, we have random thoughts, and we even say to ourselves, "How can I think this way? Why am I having such dark thoughts about something or someone: my baby, my husband, or myself?" It could be something that seems small, but is still serious, for example, jealousy, low self-esteem, or envy.

At some point, we have to ask: how can rich people who seem to have everything in this world still end up dying from drugs, suicide, depression, anxiety, and so much more? How can a woman carry her baby for nine months and end up hurting him or separating from her husband? Or how can someone appear so happy, and then all of a sudden, look lost, broken, and physically changed as if they are not the same person? Where is this depression and rage coming from? How can a person feel so low that they want to harm themselves or their baby?

You may have different answers, but thoughts are voices. Some are ours; some are God speaking through the Holy Spirit, and others are from the Devil. Which one is it? God will never give you a thought that will harm you. He is perfectly good, loving, and faithful. He cares about you, and that is why He gave His Son for you: "For God so loved the world that he gave his one and only Son, that whoever believes in him shall not perish but have eternal life" (John 3:16 NIV). It is not our desire to be depressed or full of rage. Do you wake up in the morning and say you want to be depressed? Probably not. Don't you desire to be happy and have peace every day? Probably yes.

I have heard many say, "You people see evil everywhere." The truth is, there *is* evil everywhere. For example, the CEO of one of the products you are using might be in a cult; you never know. You never know what is behind some things. You must understand that Satan will never rest. He doesn't sleep or take naps. He is working every second, sending his agents to bring disease, death, and many other ills on us.

Please, I urge you to discern the time we are in. Jesus is coming very soon, and Satan knows that. We are in warfare, so you must stay alert. Guard your thoughts and heart. Stay in thanksgiving with praise and worship. Obey the Word, serve God, and fight knowing that we already have victory through Jesus. Let me call it the way it is; it is an evil spirit deceiving people, strongholds, laughing at us because we lack knowledge, identity, and understanding of the authority God has given us. "I have given you authority to trample on snakes and scorpions and to overcome all the power of the enemy; nothing will harm you" (Luke 10:19 NIV).

Women tend to be emotional, and there are pros and cons to that, as with everything else. During pregnancy and postpartum, our emotions can feel like +100 because of the increase in hormones. Naturally, that will happen, and the Devil knows it very well. Therefore, it is important to ask God to give us, as women, the ability to control our emotions so they don't overpower us. We must also ask the Holy Spirit to lead us.

When our emotions overpower us, we tend to (or might) lose control of our thought process, which means we react immediately because we let emotions take over. Trust that emotions will come and go regularly. When that happens, and we lose control, the Enemy sees an open door, an opportunity, to bring other thoughts that weren't ours in the first place.

Now, your reaction begins to intensify. You get upset. It is normal to feel unhappy or offended by certain situations. But here is the trick of the Enemy: instead of calming down, forgiving, and choosing things that bring peace, such as praying, praising, connecting to a prayer line, worshiping, or seeking counseling, you do the exact opposite.

The Enemy will create situations or events to upset you. If he can't get to you directly, he will use people around you, like your husband, knowingly or unknowingly, to reach you. You may even ask yourself, how did we get to this point?

 You stay upset, sleep upset, and you don't forgive. Seizing another opportunity, the Enemy comes in with more thoughts, like: "Don't talk to him." "He/she was mean to you." "You just had a baby; how can he say that?" "How can he ignore it?" "Insult him." "Tell him/her that he never values you or loves you." And then guess what? You welcome those thoughts; the next thing you know, you start feeling depressed, start having rage, and so on. Those thoughts are talking to you, sometimes using your own voice.

The Devil can make you think that he is stronger and more powerful than you. Yes, he has power, but it is nothing compared to the power we have through Jesus Christ and the Holy Spirit: "You, dear children, are from God and have overcome them, because the One who is in you is greater than the one who is in the world" (1 John 4:4 NIV).

The Enemy knows his time is coming and his destiny is to burn in hell for eternity. So he wants to kill, steal, and destroy humanity, God's favorite—uniquely created in His perfect image. Since he can't and will never be able to take God's place, he wants to get rid of us. "So God created mankind in his own image, in the image of God he created them; male and female he created them" (Genesis 1:27 NIV).

Satan's mission is to deceive humanity, and he wants to trick our minds into thinking that these feelings and desires to harm are normal.

Evil spirits are very crafty at what they do. They have been on Earth for years, and they know how to deceive. We are used to letting our minds wander all over the place, giving them access, which welcomes all kinds of thoughts that our subconscious gets used to. Eventually, it becomes "normal" to think that depression, rage, and other conditions or diseases are just part of daily life. And sometimes, we even take pleasure in condemning ourselves and our brothers and sisters who struggle with depression and more.

You see a beautiful first-time mother in a store looking as if she just woke up, and people are quick to judge and laugh at her. You watch a video online of a first-time mother crying and feeling overwhelmed; again, she is judged. But how about reaching out to her and praying for her? How about kindly telling her to seek therapy or inviting her to church? How about suggesting a Christian therapist who believes in Jesus Christ as Lord and Savior and who bases their practice on the Holy Bible, someone who shares your faith? But no, many times we don't, or we simply don't care enough; we feel we have better things to do. It becomes "I and me," not you, him, or her.

We've all heard people say, "If we can help another person in need, the world will be a better place." But it's worth reflecting: what have we done to help a woman, or anyone, who is going through postpartum depression or depression? Or even something as simple as helping an elderly woman by putting her groceries in her car? Often, we may realize that we haven't. Take a moment to pause and consider what could have been done differently, something rooted in genuine love for our brothers and sisters.

Jesus reminds us in John 13:34: "A new command I give you: Love one another. As I have loved you, so you must love one another" (NIV). Love is demonstrated through action, not just words, just as God showed His love by giving His Son to save humanity.

You don't just say, "I love you," you show your love by your actions.

> Finally, believers, whatever is true, whatever is honorable and worthy of respect, whatever is right and confirmed by God's Word, whatever is pure and wholesome, whatever is lovely and brings peace, whatever is admirable and of good repute; if there is any excellence, if there is anything worthy of praise, think continually on these things [center your mind on them and implant them in your heart. (Philippians 4:8 AMP)

Any thought that goes against the Word of God is not from God. So act upon what the Bible says, and please, don't be a lukewarm believer. Are you in and out as if tomorrow is promised to you, as if you know for sure that even the next second you will still be alive? God gives us every second of our lives on this earth; that's why it's called the present. It is not to be taken for granted; it is given to us so we can work toward accomplishing our mission on Earth.

Everything starts with a thought. Whether you want to eat, sleep, or drive, you think about it first and then act upon it. Even while reading this book, you are thinking and reading at the same time. So when you allow negative thoughts, you are allowing a spirit; you are welcoming an entity to form and take place in your life for free, and to spread. Are you not aware of the thoughts that come into your mind? How do you decide what to eat? Before opening your phone to Google a food place, you have already allowed the thought of eating and what to eat to take over your mind, right? In the same way, when a negative thought comes into your mind, what do you do? Do you rebuke it in the name of Jesus, or do you simply ignore it?

Sister, ignoring a thought is not rebuking it. It is actually welcoming it. It's like saying, "Hey, I know you're here. I see you, but I'm not going to pay attention to you, so do what you want, since I didn't command you to go away." You may sense sadness, depression, frustration, and anger coming all of a sudden, maybe because something happened with your husband regarding your baby. Instead of rejecting it through praise and worship, you become pessimistic. Rather than focusing on the good, you pay attention to the bad. The good is saying,

"Father, I thank You for giving me a great husband and for allowing my child to have a dad." Instead of thanksgiving, you are complaining.

I'm not saying what your husband did was good, no. I'm saying, don't let the Enemy take control of you and your marriage. He is not only after your baby, but also your marriage because he knows what it means to God and how important it is (Ephesians 5:31-32).

What about praising God, focusing on the good, and even praying that He would soften your husband's heart, calm him, so you can discuss things later?

Sister, love and be wise.

The Bible says, "In everything give thanks to God" (Thessalonians 5:18). God didn't promise us that life would be easy, nor did He say we would be free from suffering or tribulation, but He tells us not to fear (Isaiah 41:10). He is with us, and in everything, we must give Him thanks.

Yes, sis, anything you don't deal with, whether good or bad, will eventually take control of who you are and who you will become. Depression, rage, and suicidal thoughts often enter through an open door. It's important to pause and ask yourself: which door did I leave open? Guarding your thoughts and your heart is your responsibility, not God's, because He has given you free will. So ask yourself again, where did this come from?

Any evil thought that is not rebuked in the name of Jesus will stay in your life until you deal with it. You can try any other way, but it will remain there comfortably, hiding and letting you believe who you are not: a bad mom, a bad sister, or a bad wife. Thoughts may come like these: Why can't you breastfeed your baby? Why aren't you losing weight faster? Your husband didn't compliment you today or show you affection. You might even start comparing yourself to others. Please, sister, understand that you were created uniquely in God's image. There is no one else like you.

Even thoughts of jealousy may arise, such as: who does she think she is? She's not even five months postpartum and has already lost that much weight. You may also find yourself constantly blaming others: your husband for not helping enough, complaining about the lack of sleep because the baby didn't rest, or focusing on how badly the doctor spoke to you or how big you look.

Sis, these are open doors. Complaining and blaming are some of the Enemy's tricks. Here is an important truth you must understand: the Enemy often uses facts. Yes, it is a fact that you are lacking sleep. Yes, it may be true that your husband is not helping as much as you hoped. Yes, it is a fact that you gained weight. Yes, it is a fact that your belly is bigger. Yes, it is a fact that you have stretch marks. These are facts. You can physically see that your body has changed, and that is the truth.

This is exactly how the Enemy works: he uses facts. He even

used facts and Scripture to tempt Jesus. He said, "If You are the Son of God…" (Matthew 4:3; Luke 4:3) and then quoted the Word of God. He knew that Jesus had the power to turn stones into bread, yet Jesus did not respond emotionally or impulsively. Jesus responded with the Word of God. If the Enemy used facts and Scripture to tempt Jesus, why wouldn't he try to do the same with you?

This is why discernment is so important. One way to recognize whether a thought comes from the Enemy is to examine the outcome. Ask yourself this question: What will this thought produce if I accept it and meditate on it? Will it lead to more arguments, sadness, frustration, irritation, anger, or rage? Or will it lead to compassion, love, repentance, thanksgiving, joy, praise, and worship?

The Devil does not have compassion. He does not love. He does not forgive. He does not repent. Those qualities are not in his nature. His nature is to steal, kill, and destroy. Although he may know Scripture, what he does not know and can never lead you into is love. He will never guide you toward compassion, loving thoughts, repentance, gratitude, joy, or thanksgiving. Most importantly, he will never lead you to praise and worship God when circumstances are not going as planned.

That is why, sis, you must know the Word of God to fight back. And not only know it, but also practice thanksgiving, praise, and worship daily. These serve as a barrier, a protection that prevents evil thoughts from taking root, becoming strongholds, or allowing the Enemy to enter your mind and take control. When you guard yourself this way, those thoughts will not overpower you. They will not control you. They will not have authority over you. They will not impact you in the way the Enemy intends.

Sis, overcoming postpartum is far more spiritual than physical, much more than you may realize.

The Devil can bring diseases that will blow your mind. So I urge you to understand that depression is an evil spirit (stronghold that desires to control us by controlling our though process) hiding behind thoughts, and those thoughts are not yours; they are from the Enemy: "For our struggle is not against flesh and blood, but against the rulers, against the authorities, against the powers of this dark world and against the spiritual forces of evil in the heavenly realms" (Ephesians 6:12 NIV).

As I said earlier, you may think you are battling a simple thought, but you are actually fighting an entity. If you still doubt this, there are many testimonies I encourage you to watch or listen to online.

The Devil is so stubborn that he even tempted Jesus. He knows Jesus is powerful, our Lord and Savior, the Son of God, but he still tempted Him. Be sure that the Devil will tempt us, too, at any opportunity he gets. The Bible says in Matthew 4:1-3, "Then Jesus was led by the [Holy] Spirit into the wilderness to be tempted. After He had gone without food for forty days and forty nights, He became hungry. And the tempter came and said to Him, 'If You are the Son of God, command that these stones become bread" (AMP). The Devil waited and used a moment of weakness. He knew Jesus had not eaten for forty days, and he took that opportunity to tempt Him. So be wise and fight, knowing that evil will tempt us also. It doesn't matter who we are; he knows that our flesh is weak.

Depression doesn't just start "like that." The Devil often plants a seed of doubt. He knows that when a woman gives birth naturally, her body goes through changes that impact her life. So he begins with thoughts like: "You're a bad mom. You're ugly. Your body is ugly. You can barely walk; how can you take care of your baby? You can't even cook and take care of your husband."

He will accuse and shame you: "Look at you; you have stretch marks all over your stomach and arms. What will people say about you? Hide it. You haven't showered in two days. You smell like blood. Your baby is crying, and you can't even stand up to make milk. You need to go back to working out because you are ugly, big like a balloon. Your situation will never change. The pain will remain." He repeats it: "You are ugly." Then he attacks your marriage, too: "Why are you talking to your husband like that? You should be ashamed of yourself. You don't want people to come and see what a bad mom and daughter-in-law you are. Your baby keeps crying, and you can't even help him or her stop. You can't figure out what's wrong with your baby. What a bad mom you are."

He will even call you names: "Stupid." And then he adds, "See how your husband is talking to you? It's your fault. Your baby cries because you are the problem."

The Devil is strategic. He is not smart, but he has been in this world for years, long before we were born. He has studied humans and knows exactly what to do. But he is not as strong as he seems. He is deceptive and can make you think he is more powerful than you, but he is not. God gave us the power to overcome any evil and any situation, but do you believe it? Do you believe you have the power to overcome depression, or any condition, even sickness, you are going through? How can you overcome if you allow negative thoughts to enter your mind with no resistance?

My lovely sister, God says we are His children, that we belong to Him. Our Father is the Creator of the entire world and universe, and He is in control of everything, "And he changeth the times and the seasons: he removeth kings, and setteth up kings: he giveth wisdom unto the wise, and knowledge to them that know understanding" (Daniel 2:21 KJV).

God gives us the power to destroy the Enemy. Knowing these things, why would you allow the Devil to play with your mind, life, and family?

Listen, sis, this is what the Bible says in 1 John 3:1: "See what an incredible quality of love the Father has shown to us, that we would [be permitted to] be named and called and counted the children of God! And so we are! For this reason, the world does not know us, because it did not know Him" (AMP).

Our Almighty Father also gave us authority against every attack from the Devil, and he knows that perfectly. Luke 10:19 says, "I have given you authority [that you now possess] to tread on serpents and scorpions, and [the ability to exercise authority] over all the power of the enemy (Satan); and nothing will [in any way] harm you" (AMP).

I want you to start changing the way you think about yourself. Pause for a moment and get angry at the Devil. How dare he try to play with your recovery as if you were a toy? Who does he think he is? I want you to start changing the way you think about your situation and to see it as something small, something you have already overcome and won because of who you are: a child of our almighty Father in heaven.

You are probably asking yourself, how can I change the way I think? Well, stick around. I will show you how. (Also, read the *Overcome Guide*.)

Start having thoughts of thanksgiving. Think about how good God is, how faithful He is. Start praising and worshiping God for blessing your womb. Praise Him, knowing that everything He allows is for a purpose.

Sis, if you had told me that I would end up sharing my story and writing this book by God's grace and mercy, I would have said, "Yeah, okay" lol. Today, I praise and thank God for allowing what happened to my husband and me. Oh, I do not regret it. See what God has done!

Let me remind you who you are dealing with. Satan, Lucifer, the Devil, has been here on Earth before you, me, and every other human was born. He knows that if he shows himself as the monster he truly is, we will recognize him and understand his true intentions: to destroy us. So he hides in plain sight through deception, and he starts with your flesh, through your mind.

Think and take a moment to reflect here: how did the depression start? Did it manifest just like that, or did it show up gradually? The reason therapists sit and ask you to tell them everything is that they want to know how you think, what makes you think that way, and the health of your mind. In doing so, they can help you change the way you think and perceive things. Most of the time, they hear you out, let you talk, observe your responses, and then ask more questions again and again: How? Why? When did it start? How was your childhood? How did you grow up? How is your relationship with your family? So you have to guard your mind. You must be intentional about what you allow it to think.

I want you to pause for a moment and reflect. Ask God to help you see the patterns in your mind: how, where, and when did this thought begin to take over? In reality, you know now that this is spiritual. Most likely, it entered when someone did or said something destructive. It could have also stemmed from spending too much time scrolling on social media, seeing "fit women" or "super moms" looking or dressing a certain way, or when someone spoke hurtful words to you. These things, when ignored, can open doors to a spirit of depression, rage, low self-esteem, and more. So guard your mind and heart.

If you are a "single" mother, or "single" mother-to-be, whether the dad is in the picture or not, switch the way you think, no matter what happened or how you got pregnant.

Let's remove the word "single" because you were not alone. You came from God and were created by God for God. So when I say you are not single, believe it. You were made in God's image, perfectly, by a Perfectionist (almighty God), even if your past or background tries to tell you the opposite. The world will often show you the opposite of what God says about you and your identity in Christ. Your past doesn't identify you. The way you got pregnant doesn't identify you. Rape doesn't identify you. Molestation doesn't identify you. Divorce doesn't identify you. Loss doesn't identify you. Sin in any shape or form doesn't identify you. Social media doesn't identify you. Society doesn't identify you. Even marriage doesn't identify you. Nothing else identifies you. Your identity is found in Jesus Christ, in who God says you are.

If you aspire to be a wife one day, God will give you your "half of your half" and "bone of your bones." Please, don't feel ashamed or sad, or see yourself as someone with no value. You are not less; you are valuable. What God desires for you is happiness, strength, peace, and freedom, and that freedom is found in Jesus Christ. If, while reading this, you feel convicted to give your life to Jesus Christ, skip ahead to page 118 where you can do so.

Your first Father, and the Father of your child, is God. He allows everything to happen for a reason, and what He lets happen is not to harm us. God will not allow more than we can bear. And what we experience, we will not bear it alone, but with God through the Holy Spirit. So, see your child as a blessing from God and know that He is the Father of your child. Your worldly status doesn't matter to God. What matters is that you decide to walk this path of understanding, letting Him be your Father, and believing that He is the Father of your child. No matter how you got pregnant, you are not too far from God. He will forgive you, and He is waiting for you to make Him your priority. So to God be the glory.

I applaud you because, despite the circumstances, you decided to keep your child. Trust and believe that a few months or years from now, you will glorify God for the decision you made. He has a plan for your child and for you. "For I know the plans I have for you," declares the Lord, "plans to prosper you and not to harm you, plans to give you hope and a future" (Jeremiah 29:11 NIV).

I don't know fully what you are going through, but if you put God first and surrender your all, you will never be disappointed. How can the almighty God, our Creator, disappoint you? You might not have a husband yet, and yes, it would help to have support while raising your baby, especially during postpartum, but you have God. The Holy Spirit is in you. He is your strength, your best friend, your everything. Rely on Him. He will tell you exactly what to do, where to go to get help, and even who to talk to.

Ask God to help you build a support system that He trusts for you. Trust me; He will provide. I'm not going to say it's easy to raise a child without a dad, but it is not impossible. Everything is possible with God.

Postpartum is something that is not really talked about among Christian women, married or unmarried, in our society and globally, especially in the continent of Africa. Sometimes it can be viewed as taboo, weakness, or even something shameful. Your mother may have never spoken about what can happen after giving birth, but don't blame her or feel upset. Our parents can only teach us from their experiences and what they have learned, so let's give them grace and pray for them.

I can tell you that my emotions were all over the place. I didn't really know at the time that I was going through PPT after recovering from postpartum preeclampsia. I was extremely aware of my well-being, and I did not keep my feelings to myself. I was praying, talking to God for help, and letting my husband know about these feelings. I'm grateful to God, who helped me acknowledge it before it got worse, at the right time. Otherwise, I would have gone deeper and deeper into depression.

Without even realizing it, I started saying out loud, "I don't want to go into depression. I don't want to be depressed." I said it out loud because the word "depression" doesn't sit well with me. I love peace. Even going through storms, I seek peace. Only God was able to give it to me, and He still does.

I hate the word "depression." It just sounds evil, and it is. For some people, it's almost a habit to say, "I feel so depressed today," or "I'm depressed today." No, sis, you need to stop. What is good about it? What is good about saying it, sister? Nothing. By saying it repeatedly, you are opening doors to an evil spirit, the spirit of depression, to come into your life freely. Do you really think a normal person wants to say that word or wake up in the morning having those feelings? Of course not. Everyone in this world wants peace and happiness, as mentioned before, so depression is not natural; it is spiritual (Ephesians 6:12).

So yes, depression is a spirit. Therefore, I believe that unconsciously, I was rejecting PPT (postpartum depression). I just didn't want that. I knew deep down it was spiritual. Please, think about what you are going to say before saying it. There is power in the tongue, so be careful what you say to yourself and those around you, especially your children. The Bible says in Proverbs 18:21, "Death and life are in the power of the tongue, and those who love it will eat its fruit" (NKJV). Our bodies go through various changes mentally, physically, and emotionally, so please, don't be ashamed to talk about it. Seek help. You are a precious princess of our Father in heaven, and He has all the resources to help you get through it.

As much as there are similarities, postpartum is different for many women. What happened to me might not happen to you, and vice versa. Some sisters face postpartum really well and are able to get through it, and I thank our Father in heaven for that, but for some of us, that is not the case.

My lovely sister, married or unmarried, the above still applies to all of us. If the father of your precious baby is not in the picture, or is absent for any reason, reach out. Cry out to God and get help. It is okay to reach out. Ask God to show you who you can trust to help you with your baby. I might not know exactly how hard it is, but I'm with you, sis.

God loves you regardless. You are worthy. He created you in His perfect image. "So God created mankind in his own image, in the image of God he created them; male and female he created them" (Genesis 1:27 NIV).

Science says, "Postpartum is simply what your body and your mind go through after giving birth." I suggest you do your research online or visit facilities to understand and take time to seek help. Do not disregard your feelings, thinking it will go away just like that without any help. Your well-being is an emergency that must be taken care of right away. Even if it takes time, it is a process, and I would rather you go through it with support.

I pray that our Father guides you through it. I believe that God gave us the intelligence to understand and to know what we are dealing with. Please, sis, educate yourself. I encourage you to dig for more information online; the resources out there are unlimited but be careful and wise. Not everything you see online is good. As always, talk to your primary doctor. Seek a Christian therapist, Christian counseling, and Christian marriage counseling. It does help. Remember, just because we are children of God, it does not mean we should not seek help. When we do, we must always ask God for guidance.

Chapter 7

Men Go Through Postpartum

I know you are probably thinking, "I carried a baby for nine months, gave birth, and now you're telling me that my husband goes through postpartum as well?" Yes, but differently, sis. Just because he did not carry a child for nine months or give birth does not mean he did not experience postpartum in his own way. As a woman who went through it myself, and looking back now, I can say that my husband was also dealing with it.

Most men, in general, are quiet and do not express their feelings right away. But one thing we need to understand is that your husband is human. He has a body, and that body goes through emotions. So yes, men are emotional, but in a different way. That is why it is important to know who you married: your husband's patterns and the way he processes things.

Men can get emotional and overwhelmed as well. If it is their first child, they have never taken care of a baby. They are also thinking about finances and how to provide for both of you. Your husband probably never changed or fed a baby. He may have never seen his wife give birth or experienced everything that comes with it. He has never seen you this tired, this emotional, or going through these kinds of challenges. So please, sis, give your husband grace just as God gives us grace every single second.

One version of postpartum for men is finances and the unknown: the how, when, where, and who of everything that comes with raising a child. Their "pregnancy," in a sense, becomes: how can I birth money? In other words, how can I make more money to take care of my wife and my baby, not only now, but in the long term? This is a constant concern for many men because God created them to be providers. When God gives the vision, He also provides the means to fulfill it. When God blesses you with a baby, He will also give you the ability to raise that child. Sometimes men forget this, and they do not always think about it. That is why it is also our responsibility, as wives, to help remind them that all is well, that God is in control, and that He will provide.

"And the LORD answered me, and said, Write the vision, and make it plain upon tables, that he may run that readeth it" (Habakkuk 2:2 KJV).

So remember: the vision is your baby, and the provision is God the Father. Help your husband rely on God, not only on his own ability. God gives the provision, even before the vision. Sometimes we do not discern this because we are too occupied or focused only on our own desires. But when you focus on God's desires, the provision follows, even before the vision. In this case, God has already planned for you and your baby. The question is: have you made God your first plan in your mind, body, and soul? "But seek first the kingdom of God and His righteousness, and all these things shall be added to you" (Matthew 6:33 NKJV). For example, ask God: "Lord, what is Your will regarding my baby? How can I take care of him or her? Which school? Which college? What is Your will regarding our finances? In everything, ask God to reveal His will, what He wants you to be and do as a father.

Postpartum from a Man's Perspective

Do men go through postpartum? Have we thought about it? We focus so much on ourselves during this time that we do not think about our husbands, at least some of us. And yes, it can be hard.

When I was in the hospital, my husband was very quiet. But I knew a lot was going through his mind. So, I asked him to share what he was experiencing while I was recovering and going through PPT.

Here is his point of view, a man's perspective on postpartum.

I am sharing a man's perspective on postpartum, so that you, as a woman, can go through this journey with a better understanding of what a man may experience. And for the man reading this, I want you to know that you are heard, but you are also called to be as supportive as you can be. As I write this, neither I nor you reading this is perfect. There are always areas for growth in our lives. Allow God to be in control. This is something I must continue to implement more in my own life.

The journey started from the very first day I saw my wife: meeting each other, dating and fighting, then getting married and fighting, all in love. I will go back to that part of the journey later, but for now, let's start from the moment my wife told me she was pregnant. The first thing I thought was, "Wow, we've been married for six months, and now I'm a father. Alright, let's do this."

God placed men on this earth to be providers. Unfortunately, many of us as men place our self-worth solely in our ability to provide financially. But we also have a responsibility to provide spiritually. When we lead spiritually, everything else follows: physical, emotional, mental, and even social and intellectual support to some degree.

We have a lot to carry. Fortunately, we are not meant to do it on our own; that is how God created us. Can you imagine if God made us to be completely self-sufficient, with all the resources and knowledge to obtain everything we want and need? There would be no need for God's help, and if you really think about it, no need to reproduce. Adam needed Eve, and Eve needed Adam. They also knew they needed children as they grew older. And of course, we are born fully dependent on our parents.

"The Lord God said, 'It is not good for the man to be alone. I will make a helper suitable for him... Then the LORD God made a woman from the rib He had taken out of the man, and He brought her to the man... That is why a man leaves his father and mother and is united to his wife, and they become one flesh'" (Genesis 2:18, 22, 24 NIV).

Now that my life was clearly on the path of being changed, I must admit (and my wife knew this) that I really wanted a boy. I did not realize how strong that desire was until we found out we were having a girl. As a man, and especially as the first child and son of a father who was also the first child and son, I think I simply expected the pattern to continue. It is okay that I wanted a boy, but even when our expectations feel realistic, God can have entirely different plans. In hindsight, I would advise anyone who desires a boy or a girl to truly ask God to help you be at peace with either outcome. The most important thing is that your baby is healthy. Our plans are nothing, almost laughable, compared to God's perfectly timed and executed plans. Our daughter has been such a blessing to us, and she even has my eyes, so at least I got that.

During the first phase of finding out my wife was pregnant, my mind was scrambling, how will I provide? At the time, we were living in the city where we met, but I was already ready to leave. So I was thinking, we are still leaving, but how?

Part of the reason I wanted to move, and where we chose to move, was because I wanted what I believed would be a better place to raise our daughter and future children. I was confident about leaving, but I still had doubts. God wanted this move to happen; we just did not realize it until after we moved. Once we did, things began to fall into place, including the people we met through our growing church, Impact Christian Center, Washington, among many other blessings.

So, my wife and I were attending appointments, seeing that our daughter was healthy, but here is what you came to read.

As a man, husband, and father of the household, from the pregnancy announcement to probably the first year or more of your child's life (by God's grace), the mother of your child, your wife, the woman you proposed to for better or worse, your life partner, your everything, is at her most vulnerable. This is the time when you must take an extra step as a man. Keep in mind that you are responsible for protecting her, as that is how God designed it. During this season, it is even more crucial that you give her more love. Honestly, I did not do this to the best of my ability. My biggest mistake was that I did not ask God for the strength and guidance to be the best man I could be, especially for my wife and for my daughter, who was on the way.

I reiterate that God must be at the center of our operations. As men, we can get caught up in so many things: money, food, sex, sports, hobbies, news, parents, culture, friends, relaxation, and more. That is why it is not enough to think you can do it all yourself. Sometimes we get stuck in our own heads, believing we must figure everything out alone, but we know that never truly works. In my opinion, the best thing you can do is ask God for strength and guidance. I would also suggest talking to someone, preferably a Christian-based therapist. You may be able to talk to your father or uncles if they live a life and have an approach you want to emulate. But above all, you should seek guidance from the One who has the best interest at heart for you and your family: God.

There were times when I felt overwhelmed, and you will, or probably already do, feel that way, too. I hear you. But let's take a moment to look at what your lady, your queen, is going through. Whether she is a first-time expecting mother or this is not her first child, her mind is full of thoughts. These are just a few I can think of logically and from my own experience: how will her body change during pregnancy? Will the baby be healthy? What if her husband doesn't love her the same anymore? Will her mother come and help with the baby? Why is everything getting bigger: nose, feet, and more? There are many questions she may ask herself. Your role is to ensure that you are giving her the best support you possibly can.

This does not mean buying gifts like chocolates, although that can be nice, but it primarily means listening. Listen to her when she complains about anything. Listen again, without interruption. It does not matter what the topic is. Even if she screams at you, as I said, God must fill your heart to do this. Love her anyway. Give her hugs and kisses. Show her and tell her how much you love her. Whether it is in that moment or later that day, week, or even months down the road, trust that she will appreciate it and apologize.

You can also offer quality time: taking her out to eat, going for a nice drive, or doing whatever works best for the two of you. You can offer to massage her feet; the later the pregnancy, the more you should offer, and actually do it.

Your eyes, men, are very powerful and revealing. They are a direct link to your heart's focus. There is evil everywhere in the world, but there are also acts of genuine love from God shown through people. What you choose to focus on and build with defines who you are. What am I saying? The beauty of your pregnant wife is at its highest right now. Too often, the focus stays on outer beauty, comparing wedding pictures of the woman you married to how she looks now.

Once again, God must be your guide and your strength. It is very easy to have a wandering eye. Most of the time, it is not intentional, but there are more than enough ways for the Devil to distract and confuse you. It is your responsibility to keep your heart and mind focused on your wife. Why would she feel happy or secure if you are looking at another woman, at any time, but especially while she is pregnant or recovering? Whether she sees it or not, God sees everything. Nothing is hidden from Him.

Appreciate and respect your wife for all that she is. God gave her the ability to give birth. As men, we may be built physically stronger, but God did not give us the ability to carry and deliver a child because we would not be able to handle that pain.

Eventually, your wife will give birth, but these approaches do not change. You must continue to be as supportive as possible. Now that you have your beautiful, blessed baby, there are new responsibilities: preparing bottles, changing diapers, putting the baby to sleep, washing tiny clothes, and so much more.

The hardest moments are often between 2:00 and 7:00 a.m., the deepest parts of the night. Whose turn is it to change the diaper? Who is getting up to prepare the milk? Either way, you must still carry a heart filled with God's love. Before you sleep and when you wake up, thank God for the day ahead or the day that has passed, and ask Him to fill you with His love.

You've got this, brother. You carry great responsibility, but that is because God wants to work through you, together with your wife, to build something powerful. There will be times when you say or do the wrong thing. When that happens, ask your wife for forgiveness, and then ask God for mercy. There may be "rare" times when your wife apologizes to you. Even if she does not, it is still your responsibility to forgive her and ask God to remove any unforgiveness from your heart. When you finish reading this, go give her some love. It will bless both of you.

To the woman reading this: as a man, I cannot fully understand what you are going through. All I ask is that you extend some grace to your man. There are men who have completely lost their way when their wives gave birth because they could not process what they were going through. If your man is still present, give him some credit and some love, too. I can only speak for myself. I know what helps me feel appreciated, so it is my responsibility to communicate that to my wife, but she can also ask me, so she knows.

In the same way, if you know what your husband enjoys, whether it is words of affirmation or watching his favorite baseball team, allow him that space and let him know why you are doing it. If you do not know what he prefers, ask him. Ask with a genuine heart and real focus on him. Turning the conversation back to what he is not doing for you, or why he is not immediately asking about your preferences, will defeat the purpose. If he is a good husband, he either already knows or he will bring it up because you showed care first. Have grace for him as well. As a man, I can honestly say we are very likely to make multiple mistakes. It is easy to criticize him through tone, sarcasm, words, or facial expressions, but try responding with love instead. For example, if he leaves the toilet seat up or forgets to lock the door, pause and think about what you would want to hear if you made a mistake. Then respond from that place. Trust me; he will appreciate it deeply.

As said before, your husband goes through postpartum as well, but more like a spectator sitting in the front row watching you perform at a sporting event or a gospel music concert. When he cheers for you, it is loud because he is only a few feet away. But when he is disengaged or not supportive, it can feel as though he would be better off not being there. To reiterate, your husband's role in your postpartum journey is to be as supportive as possible. This includes being more affectionate and compassionate, praying for you for strength and a healthy delivery, doing more than the "usual" while you are going through this season, and making sure that both of you are taking care of each other.

It may sound like a joke at times, but men do have emotions. Unfortunately, neither men nor women always take them seriously. Emotions can be compared to an aggressive-looking dog that has been neglected and left outside to figure things out on its own. Whether you are a man or a woman reading this, despite the "tough" image often associated with men, please consider their emotions as well. As a man, there are a few important things you should do. First, begin paying closer attention to your thoughts, and ask God to help you do this. Whenever you get negative thoughts, you have to rebuke them in Jesus' name!

"We demolish arguments and every pretension that sets itself up against the knowledge of God, and we take captive every thought to make it obedient to Christ" (2 Corinthians 10:5 NIV).

You must also ask your wife to pray for you, pray with her, and pray for her as well. This is very important. The next thing you must do is take inventory of who and what is around you.

Poison can end your life if you drink a cup of it. Now imagine pouring that same cup into an Olympic-sized swimming pool filled with fresh drinking water. Once it mixes into the water, that poison might not even make you cough. In the same way, the people you surround yourself with and the media you consume, whether social media or television, if they are negative, will eventually bring you down. You may not be able to immediately change your coworkers or your job. You definitely cannot change your family, and you may not be able to change your neighbors either. However, when it comes to the things you can remove from your life, please do so.

On the other side, increase your intake of positive influences. Become more involved in doing things for God. Ask Him how you can serve Him and His kingdom. When you spend more time helping those who are sick, sharing God's message, visiting prison inmates to give them hope, and serving others, you will begin to see how grateful you should and will be.

"Finally, brothers and sisters, whatever is true, whatever is noble, whatever is right, whatever is pure, whatever is lovely, whatever is admirable if anything is excellent or praiseworthy think about such things" (Philippians 4:8 NIV).

Let's Understand Your Husband (How a Woman Can Try to Understand Her Man)

Women, it is hard for you to fully understand what men go through. In transparency, as a man, it is not easy the other way around either. As a woman going through postpartum, you are experiencing so much that a man will never feel or fully understand. That is why, despite everything, it can be difficult for him to feel fully connected during this time, and it may be hard for him to know how to support you in the way you need.

From my experience, the best thing you can do is to give grace to one another and work together on communication. This will be one of the hardest seasons to do this, but also one of the most rewarding. The two of you need moments of honest conversation about what you want from each other and what you may not be able to give during this time, all in a place of love, not denial or resentment.

"Bear with each other and forgive one another if any of you has a grievance against someone" (Colossians 3:13 NIV).

Forgive as the Lord forgave you. Men are simple creatures in the sense that when we try to handle too many things at once, we don't function well. Unfortunately, it is easy for us to attempt to manage many responsibilities at the same time and end up overwhelmed. There are so many things we are trying to do that we fall behind without help.

You know the moment when you ask your man to bring a shirt from the upstairs room and also take the plates from the table to the kitchen downstairs? We usually hear one request or the other, so the shirt will be brought, or the plates will be taken, but seldom both. As a woman, you have the ability to be wise and build the house, so keep that in mind.

"The wise woman builds her house, but with her own hands the foolish one tears hers down" (Proverbs 14:1 NIV).

At the same time, a man deeply values being appreciated when things are done right. And when things go wrong, he values being corrected without constant nagging. This may sound like you are enabling a man to do less, but that is not the case. You are leading by example when he may be falling short, always doing so in love. However, if you are "acting nice" only to later throw it back in his face, it is better to stop right there. This is easier to practice outside of pregnancy, but being aware of it now will help you grow and do better through this season.

African Culture

Most cultures outside of America are not the strongest supporters when it comes to mental health. Unfortunately, in my culture, being from Africa, and more specifically, Nigeria, many people are stressed, not taking care of their mental health, and often no one seems to care. No matter where you are from, whether you are a woman or a man, you should make sure your mental health is attended to.

If you have a headache, the flu, a cut leg, or a broken arm, you give it the appropriate care. In the same way, when you are struggling to get through the day, going to work or dealing with a specific parent or sibling who steals your peace, you need to address it. Even if you are praying for peace, God will show you the reason or source of the unrest that is affecting you.

As mentioned above, having a true Christian therapist who can help with both spiritual and mental health issues can be beneficial. But your first therapist is God. Remember: God first. You might not even need a therapist or counseling. That is why you must seek God first and allow the Holy Spirit to guide you.

"Surely you need guidance to wage war, and victory is won through many advisers" (Proverbs 24:6 NIV).

Coming from an African upbringing, there is often an approach to postpartum that can be very detrimental to everyone involved, especially from the father's side. There are times when men expect women to fulfill traditional duties: cooking, cleaning, having sex, and more as normal or even more than possible during pregnancy and postpartum.

There needs to be a shift in mindset if you are a man. If you are reading this, you are likely among the few who either do not struggle with this issue or are actively working toward improving yourself. No matter what your culture, African or not, it is your role as a man to be as helpful as possible, even more than necessary, to your special woman during this time. You must change your mindset, if for no other reason than the fact that we are living in a time where women work outside the home while still carrying responsibilities at home. So, as a man, you can do the same. Do the home duties when it comes to cooking and cleaning. When it comes to sex, have realistic expectations as your lady is dealing with a lot.

Seeing my wife go through everything: hospital visits, weight gain, high blood pressure, fatigue, and the frustration of not being able to do simple things like bending down or putting on socks, was tough. God gave women the miraculous ability to give birth, but He did not make the process easy. Since God gave her this ability, the biggest thing I could do was be as supportive as possible, even when it meant fighting against my own selfish feelings and expectations that nothing, or not much, would change. When she needed me to get something for her or our daughter at 3 a.m., I just did it. It's because I love both of them, and that is what matters at the end of the day.

Your wife is the one going through it, and your job as a man is to be strong for her. She can see and feel your emotions from wherever she is on this journey. For me, this meant watching my wife from pregnancy through countless appointments: getting injections, scans for the baby, which was the fun part of the journey, along with sleepless nights, foot pain, not being able to reach her shoes, her hormones being all over the place, and looking in the mirror during pregnancy and postpartum, wondering if she would ever get back to where she was before.

Hopefully, you come from a good home and can ask your parents for help, learning from their experiences, what worked and what didn't. At the same time, do your own research and seek out support groups that can help. I felt deeply for my wife and everything she had to endure, so I chose to be as attentive as possible to respond to her needs, support her, and give her as much love as I could.

Chapter 8

Us – We

Marriage from God's Point of View

Marriage is not just signing a marriage license or having a big, expensive party where many people are invited. After the celebration, everyone goes back to their own lives and leaves you to yours. Marriage is more than that. It is a divine institution.

Marriage is giving yourself up, just as Jesus gave Himself up for the church as a spouse. The Bible says: "Husbands, love your wives, just as Christ loved the church and gave himself up for her to make her holy, cleansing her by the washing with water through the word, and to present her to himself as a radiant church, without stain or wrinkle or any other blemish, but holy and blameless" (Ephesians 5:25-27 NIV).

Marriage is a relationship that is not only built through joy, money, vacations, and celebrations, but also through pain, sorrow, sacrifice, sickness, and hardship. You are there to serve, not only to receive. You are there to build together and to work toward God's mission. Jesus gave Himself on the cross for the church without worrying about whether we would choose Him, love Him in return, or receive Him as our Lord and Savior. Marriage is giving yourself up, most times putting yourself last, for your spouse, no matter their imperfections.

Yes, marriage is beautiful and has many benefits, but we should not be quick to break that covenant when things go wrong. Seek help when your spouse is going through a difficult time, and do not be quick to even think about divorce or leaving, let alone acting on it. Only when a life is in danger should separation be considered. Even then, in every situation, good and especially bad, seek God's guidance so you do not make a decision you will regret. If you try to do things your way and not God's way, you can destroy yourself. Never end your life for your spouse. That is not God's will for you. Seek help and do not remain silent.

Marriage is about building intimacy with Jesus. Let us read what God says in: Revelation 19:7-9:

> Let us rejoice and be glad and give him glory! For the wedding of the Lamb has come, and his bride has made herself ready. Fine linen, bright and clean, was given her to wear... [Fine linen stands for the righteous acts of God's holy people.] Then the angel said to me, 'Write this: Blessed are those who are invited to the wedding

supper of the Lamb!' And he added, 'These are the true words of God.' (NIV)

I recommend reading *Four Secrets of Successful Marriage* by Yvan Castanou. The Lamb is Jesus, married to the church, and the church is us: you, me, and all His true believers. Marriage is not just a feeling; it is a decision to stay with someone until death. Jesus did not decide by feelings, but by obedience and love that cannot be explained, love that endures hardship and wins battles. This supernatural love is called *agape* love.

Agape love is found in God. Have you ever wondered how some couples remain married for many years, or even a few, and still go through everything together while remaining joyful and deeply in love? It is not because it is easy. It is because they understood the true meaning of marriage. They accepted and practiced the agape love of God, and in doing so, they honored Him.

We commit to our spouses just as Jesus committed Himself to the church, not because we are sinless or always obedient (for we all sin and must ask God daily for forgiveness and cleansing by the blood of Jesus), but because God knows we need Him. We need God's help. Living life without His guidance makes it difficult to thrive in this broken world. We need to be united with His Son, Jesus, to fulfill our mission on Earth. Your spouse can help you fulfill that mission, and the Devil knows this. That is why he works so hard to destroy marriages and families. A broken home leads to broken children, and broken children often become broken adults.

Do not base your marriage on feelings alone, but on a divine institution that must be honored.

"Let marriage be held in honor among all, and let the marriage bed be undefiled, for God will judge the sexually immoral and adulterous" (Hebrews 13:4 NIV).

When you understand what marriage truly is, your perspective on challenges will change. God created marriage from the beginning. It started with Adam and Eve. God saw that something was missing when He created Adam. You have likely heard this vow many times: "For better or for worse, until death do us part." It means exactly what it says, no explanation needed. Scripture confirms this.

"A woman is bound to her husband as long as he lives. But if her husband dies, she is free to marry anyone she wishes, but he must belong to the Lord" (1 Corinthians 7:39 NIV).

You cannot give up on each other when things become difficult.

We Are One

When God created Adam, He knew and saw that something was missing; Adam was not complete, and something was not right. It says in Genesis 2:20, "So the man gave names to all the livestock, the birds in the sky, and all the wild animals. But for Adam no suitable helper was found" (NIV). God said in Genesis 2:18, "It is not good for the man to be alone. I will make a helper suitable for him" (NIV).

Let us stop seeing ourselves as individuals married to other individuals. Rather, you and your spouse are one. The fact that, after all the things God gave Adam, it was still not enough, shows us something powerful. Adam may have felt lonely. Something was missing. He was not complete. He may not have known what was missing, but God knew exactly that Adam needed a helper, a wife.

Listen, sister and brother, before you were born, GOD knew you would need a helper and a provider. He created you in His perfect image. God made a perfect woman using Adam's bone and flesh, almost like making twins, alike, so that Adam would not look elsewhere. She was a perfect human being created only for Adam, not comparable to any other being. With her, Adam was complete and fulfilled. God made sure Adam was asleep because this perfection needed to be created in secret and with the same DNA. Adam and Eve needed to share the same vision, similar interests, and the same purpose in life. Have you ever seen a couple that looks alike, acts alike, and seems genuinely perfect for each other, like they were meant to be together? God gives you the one who completes you. He knows what you need and when you need your flesh of your flesh and bone of your bones.

God says in Genesis 2:21-23, "So the Lord GOD caused the man to fall into a deep sleep; and while he was sleeping, He took one of the man's ribs and then closed up the place with flesh. Then the Lord GOD made a woman from the rib He had taken out of the man, and He brought her to the man. The man said, 'This is now bone of my bones and flesh of my flesh; she shall be called "woman," for she was taken out of man'" (NIV).

Here, we see that even though we view and approach things differently as men and women, and we like different things, we are one body, mind, and spirit. As soon as we get married, let us stop focusing only on ourselves and our own needs. Instead, let us focus on each other's needs and desires. Your pain is mine. Your joy is mine. Your sorrow is mine. Your postpartum is mine. I will be with you through everything. You are not alone. Your debt is my debt. Your finances are mine. Your peace and joy are what I pursue and ask God for in our lives. Your sickness is mine because I was made by God and for you. I am all yours.

"For this reason a man will leave his father and mother and be united to his wife, and the two will become one flesh" (Ephesians 5:31 NIV).

So, dearest husband, your wife needs you the most during this postpartum phase. She needs your love, peace, and strength because you need the same. You cannot accomplish God's purpose in your life without her. Your wife's peace, joy, and love must be your daily desire because by helping her, you are helping yourself. You are one. It is your duty to care for her. She did not search for you; just as Adam needed a helper, you also needed her. That is why your desire to be married was granted by God, and He gave you your perfect flesh of your flesh and bone of your bones.

Who Is Your Husband?

Your husband is the head of the house; that is why God created Adam first. His mission is to work and take care of the household. The Bible says in Genesis 2:15, "The Lord GOD took the man and put him in the Garden of Eden to work it and take care of it" (NIV). This does not mean that because he is the head of the household, you have no value. Even as the head of the house, he still needs a helper because there are things men naturally cannot do; they are limited in certain areas. I'm sure you've noticed that in some areas, your husband simply cannot do things the way you do. Even after showing him several times, he still may not get it.

Men do not naturally multitask; they must learn, and even then, they often cannot do it the way women do. Men provide for the house, but they do not build a home. He provides and cares for it, but the one who builds the home is you, my sister. Your man comes with a vision and a purpose, and it is your duty to help him fulfill it. The Bible says in Proverbs 14:1, "The wise woman builds her house, but with her own hands the foolish one tears hers down" (NIV).

This means that as women, we are powerful. We can help our husbands succeed in everything God has placed in their hearts. We can take great care of our children and our homes. At the same time, we can work, build businesses, and still serve the Lord daily. We can overcome mountains that stand against us. We can forgive and move forward. Women, we are perfect. We were perfectly made by God in secret. We are powerful. However, it is also our duty to submit to our husbands, as stated in 1 Peter 3:1:

> In the same way, you wives, be submissive to your own husbands [subordinate, not as inferior, but out of respect for the responsibilities entrusted to husbands and their accountability to God, and so partnering with them], so that even if some do not obey the word [of God], they may be won over [to Christ] without discussion by the godly lives of their wives. (AMP)

Submission

> Submit to one another out of reverence for Christ. Wives, submit yourselves to your own husbands as you do to the Lord. For the husband is the head of the wife as Christ is the head of the church, His body, of which He is the Savior. Now as the church submits to Christ, so also wives should submit to their husbands in everything. (Ephesians 5:21-24)

Submission does not mean weakness. Rather, it means respecting your husband in his God-given role as the head of the home, following the example of the church's submission to Christ as its head. In the same way, allowing your husband to be the leader in the home means letting him make decisions, take charge, and trusting his leadership. This does not mean that you cannot express yourself or share your thoughts. It means you can come alongside him and offer advice. Help him as he leads, even when he makes mistakes, and you, sis, do your part while letting God be the judge. A good man of God will actually ask his wife for help and guidance because he understands the power and wisdom his wife carries. He understands that she is his flesh and bones.

It means respecting God for giving men authority as leaders, providers, and carriers of responsibility. Have you not heard a woman say, "I like a man who knows what he wants, a man who can protect and provide, who cares for me?" A powerful man does not lead by control but by direction, knowing where he is going in life, a leader of men. No woman wants a man who stays at home and does nothing.

Listen, sis, sometimes I like it when my husband takes charge and makes decisions. I like when my husband leads and tells me what to do (not dictates). I like it when my husband teaches me things that I don't know. Don't you?

There is a reason why God created Adam first. While making Adam, God gave him vision, the ability to work, to take care of the animals, and to provide for the family. Sometimes it can be hard for men to do other things because it's not their duty or calling. That is why we need to understand what men can and cannot do from God's point of view.

God created Adam and gave him everything, but He observed and saw that something was missing. If you are aspiring to get married, please wait patiently. God is making your Adam. Also, ask God what you desire your husband to be like, believing that He hears you. That was my prayer.

How God Showed Me My Husband

I told God exactly what I was looking for in my future husband. I remember praying about it and telling Him that I would wait until He showed me. I did have a couple of men propose to me for marriage, but I believed God would show me, so I waited. That man, my calm, loving, tall husband, whom I love, at that time was actually my friend and business partner. Yes, sis, he was always there, lol. I would see him every Tuesday and Friday at our business meetings. He was, and still is, so funny and such a gentleman. I thank God for my husband.

One day, as I was getting out of the car and fixing my dress to go into a business meeting, I felt something, or someone, poke my heart. It felt physical, yet spiritual. I can't fully explain it with words, but I truly felt it. Then I heard a voice say, "Look." I looked up and saw my husband coming toward the outside door with a big smile, lol, smiling at me, and I said, "God, that's Him." I had no hesitation. So yes, sis, if you aren't married yet, ask God. He will give you more than you expect to receive. Glory be to God.

Who Is Your Wife?

Your wife is not your provider; that is not God's mission for her. She is not a sexual object, nor someone meant only to multiply children. She is not beneath you, and she is not above you. Rather, she is your helper, your flesh and your bones, your peace and your joy. She is there to help you in areas where you are weak or simply cannot function on your own. She is rare gold, a sapphire that God created while you were sleeping. She is full of hidden treasures that will help you prosper.

Just like Adam, you cannot live fully without your wife. If your calling is marriage, then you must be married; otherwise, you would not have had the desire to marry in the first place. God does not give desires without purpose. After a long day at work, you need and desire her love. You long to come home to a peaceful environment where there is food, joy, and rest. Your wife is a divine mystery, created in secret just for you.

Adam did not see how God made Eve. This is because a woman's power and ability cannot be fully understood by a man; it must be honored by her husband. Your wife can make you the happiest man in the world. On the flip side, she can make you the most miserable. That is why God gives clear instructions to husbands:

> In the same way, you husbands, live with your wives in an understanding way [with great gentleness and tact, and with an intelligent regard for the marriage relationship], as with someone physically weaker, since she is a woman. Show her honor and respect as a fellow heir of the grace of life, so that your prayers will not be hindered or ineffective. (1 Peter 3:7 AMP)

"Physically weaker" does not mean weak. It means she was designed to be protected, loved, acknowledged, uplifted, and appreciated daily. Even though a woman can love herself, she still needs her husband to affirm and validate her consistently. She needs affection because, without it, intimacy dies. Romance matters.

Respect means being appreciated and never taken for granted. She wants to be cherished at home and honored in public. She wants to be seen, valued, and celebrated, and yes, sometimes she wants to be the center of your attention. That is what respect looks like to women.

Men, if you desire your wife to submit to you, you must do your part. A happy wife is a happy man; that saying is true. A woman has the power to either build your life or tear it down. Women often see things from a distance that men cannot, and that is why God took His time creating us while Adam slept.

It was a woman who influenced Samson. It was a woman who convinced Adam to eat the fruit. And it was a woman, Esther, who persuaded a king not to destroy the Jewish people. Ruth and Esther were wise women.

Women have the capacity to destroy or build. So, husband, ask yourself: where do you expect your wife to receive her affection from? Yes, God can and will give her everything, but she also needs it from you. You are her protector. This is what God says:

> Husbands, love your wives, just as Christ loved the church and gave himself up for her to make her holy, cleansing her by the washing with water through the word, and to present her to himself as a radiant church,

without stain or wrinkle or any other blemish, but holy and blameless. In this same way, husbands ought to love their wives as their own bodies. He who loves his wife loves himself. After all, no one ever hated their own body, but they feed and care for their body, just as Christ does the church. (Ephesians 5:25-32)

Let's Overcome Postpartum Together

Looking back at my story, I can tell you that I thought I had to go through it with God and by myself. I didn't have the revelation that my husband and I are actually one. Now, I understand that we made this baby together and must go through this postpartum season together. We are connected, just like Adam and Eve.

Listen, sis, you are the one dealing with so much mentally and physically. You carried your baby for nine months or more. After birth, your body changes, and your mental health may not feel stable enough. However, you must also acknowledge that your husband has been dealing with this mentally since the moment you told him you were pregnant.

So let's see how we can get through this together with God. Let's be more understanding and open to listening, even when we don't agree with certain things, whether it's something your husband is saying or the way he is acting. Let's not be quick to judge or react. Let's start asking God for the ability and the strength to work together as one.

I know how easy it is to tell your husband that he is doing something wrong: carrying the baby the wrong way, not knowing how to calm or bathe the baby. Please, let's give each other grace (that is my husband's favorite word to say whenever we have a disagreement). No one is perfect. Sometimes, he may not do things the "right" way, but you need him, and he needs you.

You need his affection even more. You need his help even more. You need his validation even more. But let's also understand that your husband is struggling, too, and he needs you as well. This is a huge change. You may not know how to love or care for him right now, and you're not doing it on purpose. You are tired. I understand. So talk to him in a calm space or seek therapy together instead of alone. Pray together and find ways to attend doctor's appointments together.

Listen Brother

I respect you, but let's be honest and speak facts. Because your wife carries and gives birth to your baby, you should not ignore her when she is acting a certain way. When she is screaming, overwhelmed, or exhausted, you must understand that she is extremely tired. She has gone through major changes physically and in her feminine areas. She may be thinking, after this, am I going to satisfy my husband? What will our sex life be like? She might not even feel comfortable being naked in front of you. The Enemy knows this, so he tries to distort how she looks or behaves in your presence.

You must understand that overcoming postpartum requires both of you working together with God. You both said, for better or for worse, right? In sickness and in poverty, right? Until death do us part. So stop seeing postpartum as only a woman's issue and not a man's. Let's stop ignoring men's feelings. Let's stop assuming that she "has it," that she can go to therapy, counseling, or the hospital alone because she is strong. That thinking is wrong. What about you going with her to therapy?

You might say, "No, I'm not dealing with postpartum." Well, brother, you are. You are thinking about how to provide for your baby. You are working double shifts or worrying about job security. You miss being intimate with your wife. You feel like your wife is giving all her attention to the baby and not to you. You may have witnessed the birth of your child, and that experience may have affected you. You are sleep-deprived. You don't know how to care for your wife because she is going through so much more than you. You miss going on dates with your wife. You see your wife bleeding and don't know what to do. You are afraid your baby might get hurt if you carry him or her. Your wife may constantly tell you what to do or how to be a husband, and sometimes you don't like it because of pride. You may even question in your mind whether you love your wife and your baby. Any of these, and more, are signs that you, too, may be experiencing postpartum and possibly depression. But it takes a real man, a Husband with a capital H, to humble himself, admit it, and open up to his wife.

I believe you are that man. You just don't know what to do yet, and that is normal. Don't be ashamed. Be encouraged. This is where overcoming postpartum together begins. You will both find joy in your recovery, and the Enemy will have no say. You are also learning to adjust to your new life physically, mentally, emotionally, and in every other way.

"However, each one of you also must love his wife as he loves himself, and the wife must respect her husband" (Ephesians 5:33 NIV).

My brother, by now, you have read enough to know that this is a vital time in your wife's life, whether she is in the pregnancy stage or the postpartum part of her journey. Take the time to truly understand your woman. It is best if you are already doing this when she is not pregnant, so it becomes a habit. If you are not, then now is the time to do so more than ever. Make sure to go back to biology and understand, scientifically, what is happening. Most importantly, ask God for strength, guidance, and understanding because that is the greatest and most necessary step you can take.

When you understand her physically, mentally, and spiritually, things will still be tough. However, they will be easier because you have a clearer understanding of what is going on. You must also do the same on your side by knowing your own role. As a man, you carry the responsibility to provide. Whether this is your first time experiencing pregnancy or not, your responsibilities as a provider are increasing. Take the time to understand what other men are going through. Look into the science but also have honest discussions with your wife about how you are both feeling and how you can support each other, remembering that, during this season, you will be supporting her even more.

Chapter 9

The Key to Enter Heaven

If you are a born-again Christian, then this is a refresh, a reminder to keep pursuing your relationship with God and not to give up your faith for this world. If you are simply curious, or for any other reason, you read all the way to this final chapter, I believe there was a small voice whispering in your ear to keep reading. Even if there is another voice telling you the opposite, and you feel you have heard nothing at all, I encourage you to stay until the end.

Why Talk About Salvation

You may be wondering why I am talking about Jesus. The answer is simple: He is our Lord and Savior, our Deliverer, who sacrificed Himself for us. He paid the price for our sins, for all humanity, so that we would not perish but have eternal life with our Father and with Him. As born-again Christians, it is our duty, our mission, to spread the gospel. It would be selfish not to speak about salvation, and it would not honor God.

As someone who was once lost, broken, afraid, sick, oppressed, molested, and abused, I can honestly say the Enemy used and attacked me for over twenty years. But by the grace and mercy of God, when I gave my life to Jesus, I was delivered. I am free. I have peace, life, and love in abundance. I now live with purpose and a mission to accomplish for our heavenly Father. So I cannot stay quiet. I want that for you. I enjoy talking about the One who died for my sins without deserving it or asking Him to do so.

Let me ask you something: would you die for someone else's sins? Would you carry all their condemnation, generational curses, and sicknesses? Let's be honest; the answer is no. So I hope that question has been answered. But you may still be wondering if Jesus did all of this for us, why are we still suffering in the world? The answer is simple: choice.

We live in an imperfect world filled with evil because of the Devil. He wanted to be God, and he, along with his angels, was cast out of heaven to the earth. But God sent us a Savior, our Lord Jesus Christ, and through Him, we have authority over all evil.

Jesus carried everything for us: the suffering that comes from within and the suffering that comes from outside. What is inside our hearts, brokenness, sadness, weariness, often reflects outwardly. That is why God tells us in Proverbs 4:23, "Above all else, guard your heart, for everything you do flows from it" (NIV). The Enemy knows this, so he begins by attacking our minds with false, deceptive, and destructive thoughts. Humanity chose to reject Jesus.

There were multiple points in our lives, probably multiple times today, even within the last hour before you were reading, when we heard the name of Jesus or thought about doing something for Him. Did you pass someone on the street who looked different and **chose** not to say hello from a place of love? Did you play music from your favorite artist who sings about sex, drugs, or things God wants you to stay away from, rather than listening to or singing a gospel song? Did you scream at someone: your spouse, colleague, child, or anyone else, instead of reacting with peace, love, and understanding as Jesus would?

You could have heard about Jesus in different ways. Maybe it was on the street through someone preaching, through a song, or through a billboard or sign saying, "Jesus Loves You." But did you welcome Him into your heart? No, right? You probably rejected Him or said something like, "Jesus doesn't exist," right? So you have had multiple opportunities to decide between Jesus and the Devil, but you chose the things of this world. That is why you are still suffering because you chose the wrong one: the Devil.

God saw that you were suffering and going through difficult times, so He sent His Son, Jesus, to save, heal, protect, love, carry, and provide for you, and you still rejected Him.

When Jesus comes into your life, He takes away the suffering from the inside and changes you forever, throughout eternity. It is not just a three-month peace, joy, and power, but a lasting peace and joy, even when evil surrounds us. Listen, our Father is so loving that He allows you to choose. He does not force you to choose His Son, Jesus Christ. If you allow people to keep telling you lies, then you will be disappointed.

Your Choice

So, let's reflect on the questions below:

- Who are you going to choose?
- If you don't choose Jesus, where are you going after this life?

Oh, you said the universe? I ask, where in the universe? I don't think you want to find out when you are already dead because there will be no going back. You will call on Jesus, and He will not answer because when He knocked on the door of your heart, you closed it and rejected Him. So do not let your ego pull you away from God. It leads to hell.

Where Are You Going After Death?

We tend to live this life without wondering what will happen tomorrow. We think that we are in control of how our bodies function. I have asked myself if I were to die today, where would I go? So let me ask you directly: when your time comes, knowing it can be at any moment, where are you going? Are you 100 percent sure that you will go somewhere peaceful, filled with pure love, peace, and joy? And how do you know that you will go to heaven and not hell?

I'm sure you may have seen many testimonies on YouTube or TikTok about people who went to heaven or hell, people who died and came back to life, and were never the same again; they became new beings. If you have not watched them or if you have doubts, go and see for yourself. Stop following what everyone else is saying or asking and be your own judge for once. Call upon the name of Jesus, who is always waiting for your call.

Jesus, the Son of God

Who is Jesus Christ, the Son of God? He is God. John 14:11 says, "Believe me that I am in the Father and the Father is in me, or else believe on account of the works themselves" (ESV). John 3:16 tells us, "For God so loved the world that he gave his one and only Son, that whoever believes in him shall not perish but have eternal life" (NIV).

This is how God the Father shows His love to us, by giving a part of Himself, who came through a virgin woman named Mary as a holy human. "To a virgin espoused to a man whose name was Joseph, of the house of David; and the virgin's name was Mary" (Luke 1:27 KJV). She conceived through the Holy Spirit and gave birth to Him in a humble place. Luke 2:7–8 says, "She wrapped him in cloths and placed him in a manger, because there was no guest room available for them. And there were shepherds living out in the fields nearby, keeping watch over their flocks at night."

The Way, the Truth, and the Life

"Jesus said to him, 'I am the way, and the truth, and the life. No one comes to the Father except through me'" (John 14:6 ESV).

Jesus is the way to heaven and not hell. He is the right road, the guidance you have been asking for. Jesus is the truth you have been wanting to know for so long: your true identity, your true self, the purpose of your existence. Jesus is the reason you are still alive. He will fill that empty soul of yours with love, peace, and joy. He will wipe away your tears, sorrows, and fears. There is no other way but through Him.

The Sacrificed Lamb

God sent His Son, Jesus Christ, for a reason: to give up His life for us so that we would be set free, delivered, healed, and have eternal life. I searched the Bible to understand exactly what Jesus did for us, so that you may know the situations you are in are not the will of God. The pain, sadness, sickness, and suffering you are experiencing are not your portion. You are not meant to suffer and live in pain for the rest of your life, but to have eternal peace.

"Surely he took up our pain and bore our suffering, yet we considered him punished by God, stricken by him, and afflicted. But he was pierced for our transgressions, he was crushed for our iniquities; the punishment that brought us peace, and with his wounds we are healed" (Isaiah 53:4-5 NIV).

You are not meant to stay lost, wondering what your life is about or where you are going. This is not your fault.

> We all, like sheep, have gone astray, each of us has turned to our own way; and the Lord has laid on him the iniquity of us all. He was oppressed and afflicted, yet he did not open his mouth; he was led like a lamb to the slaughter, and as a sheep before its shearers is silent, so he did not open his mouth. By oppression and judgment he was taken away. Yet who of his generation protested? For he was cut off from the land of the living; for the transgression of my people he was punished. He was assigned a grave with the wicked, and with the rich in his death, though he had done no violence, nor was any deceit in his mouth. Yet it was the Lord's will to crush him and cause him to suffer, and though the Lord makes his life an offering for sin, he will see his offspring and prolong his days, and the will of the Lord will prosper in his hand. (Isaiah 53:6-10 NIV)

After taking away our suffering and sins, He carried darkness out of our lives and brought us into the light before our Father.

> After he has suffered, he will see the light of life and be satisfied; by his knowledge my righteous servant will justify many, and he will bear their iniquities. Therefore I

will give him a portion among the great, and he will divide the spoils with the strong, because he poured out his life unto death, and was numbered with the transgressors. For he bore the sin of many, and made intercession for the transgressors. (Isaiah 53:11-12 NIV)

After reading what our Lord and Savior Jesus did for us, you cannot tolerate any form of sin or condemnation controlling your life like a puppet. You must seek Him if you have not fully given your life to Him. It is never too late to do so, but once your time comes, it will be. God is giving you a second chance, and this is your reminder to take it.

The Blood of Jesus

"But God demonstrates his own love for us in this: While we were still sinners, Christ died for us. Since we have now been justified by his blood, how much more shall we be saved from God's wrath through him!" (Romans 5:8-9 NIV).

There are witches who perform blood sacrifices because they understand that there is power, life and death, in the blood. Leviticus 17:11 says, "For the life of the flesh is in the blood, and I have given it to you on the altar to make atonement for your souls; for it is the blood that makes atonement by the life." It is unfortunate that some followers of Jesus Christ neglect the truth that the blood of Jesus cleanses and purifies us from all sin.

There is no such thing as a "small" or "big" sin because sin is sin in God's eyes. Someone who tells a white lie about eating another person's food and denies it is a sinner in the eyes of God just as much as someone who commits mass murder or openly worships the Devil. Regardless of the sin, the blood of Jesus cleanses and purifies the moment you give your life to Jesus Christ.

"But if we walk in the light, as he is in the light, we have fellowship with one another, and the blood of Jesus, his Son, purifies us from all sin" (1 John 1:7 NIV).

"Since we have now been justified by his blood, how much more shall we be saved from God's wrath through him!" (Romans 5:9 NIV).

The Blood of Jesus Redeems and Forgives Us

The blood of Jesus redeems us from slavery and bondage. No matter what has been keeping you from fulfilling God's destiny for your life, in Him, you have been redeemed

"In him we have redemption through his blood, the forgiveness of sins, in accordance with the riches of God's grace" (Ephesians 1:7 NIV).

The Blood of Jesus Breaks Generational Curses

It does not matter what generational curses have been destroying you or your family. Jesus canceled them and paid the price with His blood. No matter the condition you are in, through Him, you are redeemed.

"Christ redeemed us from the curse of the law by becoming a curse for us, for it is written: 'Cursed is everyone who is hung on a pole'" (Galatians 3:13 NIV).

The Blood of Jesus Sanctifies Us and Gives Us Victory

Demons have no power or authority the moment you give your life to Jesus. You have victory through His blood. It is important to understand this because Jesus already won the battle on the cross. The victory is already ours, and we must remind the Devil of it.

"They triumphed over him by the blood of the Lamb and by the word of their testimony; they did not love their lives so much as to shrink from death" (Revelation 12:11 NIV).

"And having disarmed the powers and authorities, he made a public spectacle of them, triumphing over them by the cross" (Colossians 2:15 NIV).

"And by that will, we have been made holy through the sacrifice of the body of Jesus Christ once for all" (Hebrews 10:10 NIV).

The Holy Spirit

When Jesus appeared to His disciples and told them that He had to leave and go to the Father (John 16:5), I wonder what was going through their minds. Can you imagine being led, fed, and protected by someone visible, and then suddenly being told that He must go away for a little while? I believe they were sad, and more. John 16:6 says, "But because I have said these things to you, sorrow has filled your heart" (NKJV). But Jesus told them that He had to go so He could send someone to help them: "Nevertheless I tell you the truth. It is to your advantage that I am going away; for if I do not go away, the Helper will not come to you; but if I depart, I will send Him to you" (John 16:7 NKJV).

I remember when I came back home and was recovering from postpartum preeclampsia while battling depression. I constantly heard two voices: one telling me lies and the other telling me the truth. I knew the lies were from the Devil (as I said before, it starts with a thought in our minds), and the other voice, who was it? You know the answer. Yes, you got it right, the Holy Spirit.

I'm sure all of us have had moments when we wanted to do something wrong, but a voice told us to stop and not do it, right? Who do you think that is? Listen, the Devil will never tell you to stop harming yourself or doing something bad. Remember, he is the king of lies and deception. He hates humankind deeply; it doesn't even make sense. That is why the help of the Holy Spirit is so powerful.

If you are a born-again Christian, you already have the Holy Spirit. He is in us, with us, and upon us. Let's learn about the Holy Spirit: "And that is what some of you were. But you were washed, you were sanctified, you were justified in the name of the Lord Jesus Christ and by the Spirit of our God" (1 Corinthians 6:11 NIV).

Helper

The Holy Spirit is in us, with us, and upon us. He is a part of us, our best friend, who will never disappoint us. I'm sure you have heard people say, "Never say never" because you never know what might happen. But in this case, the Holy Spirit will never disappoint us, forsake us, or hurt us. Some people say they have physically experienced the presence of the Holy Spirit as if He were right next to them like a person. Because of this, I believe that He is not only a Spirit, but also a Person. The Holy Spirit is here to help us in our walk with Christ. Without Him, just like the disciples, there is nothing we can do or say that will truly please God.

"Nevertheless I tell you the truth. It is to your advantage that I go away; for if I do not go away, the Helper will not come to you; but if I depart, I will send Him to you" (John 16:7 NKJV).

The Holy Spirit is here to help us, no matter the situation. He can lead us out of any danger if we obey Him and surrender our daily lives to His guidance.

Revealer and Guide

The Holy Spirit is a gentleman. He is present, but He will not force you to do what you do not want to do. Allow Him to guide and lead you, and you must obey, even when you do not fully understand why. Sometimes He may not tell us everything right away, or He may not explain at all. But we must remember that He is the Spirit of God, and just as we obey God, we must obey Him. Otherwise, we may find ourselves going in circles, unsure of what we are doing or where we are going.

"But when he, the Spirit of truth, comes, he will guide you into all the truth. He will not speak on his own; he will speak only what he hears, and he will tell you what is yet to come" (John 16:13 NIV).

"And when He has come, He will convict the world of sin, and of righteousness, and of judgment" (John 16:8 NKJV).

"Though I have been speaking figuratively, a time is coming when I will no longer use this kind of language but will tell you plainly about my Father" (John 16:25 NIV).

There are certain things we cannot comprehend without the Holy Spirit. That is why some people do not understand us.

Intercedes and Prays for Us

The Holy Spirit helps us pray. Sometimes when it is time to pray, we do not know what to say or how to say it. Then suddenly, we feel inspired and find ourselves praying for thirty minutes or even an hour, knowing very well that we could not have done that on our own. Some of us even dream that we are praying while asleep. It is not us; it is the Holy Spirit interceding for us.

"In the same way, the Spirit helps us in our weakness. We do not know what we ought to pray for, but the Spirit himself intercedes for us through wordless groans. And he who searches our hearts knows the mind of the Spirit, because the Spirit intercedes for God's people in accordance with the will of God" (Romans 8:26-27 NIV).

"He will glorify Me, for He will take of what is Mine and declare it to you. All things that the Father has are Mine. Therefore I said that He will take of Mine and declare it to you" (John 16:14-15 NKJV).

Prayer of Salvation

After reading this, if you want to get to know Jesus and have a personal relationship with Him and our Father in heaven, even if you are curious or skeptical, open your heart and pray this with me. Say it out loud or in your heart. Just believe that God is here, and that He is filled with joy to see and hear you coming to Him.

Say out loud:

My Lord and Savior, Jesus Christ, I repent of all my sins. Please forgive me. I surrender my life to You. Wash me clean with Your blood. I receive and believe that Jesus Christ is the Son of our almighty God, that He died on the cross for my sins and rose again. I believe in my heart and confess with my mouth that Jesus is my Lord and Savior, and that He reigns forever and ever. Amen.

The Bible says there is a glorious celebration in heaven over one sinner who repents, so God is having a big celebration in heaven just for you: "I tell you that in the same way there will be more rejoicing in heaven over one sinner who repents than over ninety-nine righteous persons who do not need to repent" (Luke 15:7 NIV).

Welcome back home, dear sister and brother!

Conclusion

Before saying, touching, or doing anything, think first. It is important to recognize your thoughts. When a thought does not reflect love, remember that love comes from our Father because the Devil has no love in him. He knows the Bible, but there is nothing good or lovely about darkness or evil. Because of this, he knows only parts of the Word, not the heart of God. That is why I urge you to truly reflect on the kind of thoughts you have daily.

If you have thoughts of low self-esteem, suicide, shame, anger, violence, loneliness, hatred, or any form of harming yourself, those are not your original thoughts, and they are not from God. He does not desire you to think this way. You are His precious child and daughter. It is impossible for Him to want harm for you.

"Do not be conformed to this world, but be transformed by the renewing of your mind" (Romans 12:2 NIV).

The Devil is a master of lies and deception. Nowadays, you can see how he works, but many people still cannot recognize it. Why?

Because he controls our minds when we allow him to. He convinces us that it is okay to hate, okay to feel constantly sad, okay to feel a little depressed, okay to smoke, and okay to drink. He tells us it is okay to fight, to insult others, to even hate our Father, and Christians. But it is not entirely your fault. Just like me, you have been lied to.

Now, you have the opportunity to say, enough is enough. That is not who I am. Those thoughts are not mine. Postpartum depression, or any form of depression, is not from me. I reject and rebuke the spirit of depression in the name of Jesus. Amen. If you feel conviction, or even uncertainty, repeat the Prayer of Salvation on the preceding page. Let Jesus Christ come into your life, and it will never be the same again.

This journey reflects the reality of what many women experience when we bring life into the world. The good part is that it does not have to be miserable. You do not have to feel pressured to look good within a week. You do not have to go through it alone. Remember, you have your husband and God first on your side. He has given you the Holy Spirit to guide and help you in everything, yes, everything, not only when you pray, but in every area of your life.

Looking back, even during postpartum, I thank God I went through it. God wanted me to be one of His voices to expose and denounce the tricks of the Enemy who lies to you.

Let's Talk About You

I am building a community of women who support one another through this journey, and I want you to be a vital part of it. As sisters in Christ, we are called to support each other by the grace of God. Whether you choose to share your full story, share only what you are comfortable with, or simply be part of a Christ-centered sisterhood that offers prayer and encouragement during your postpartum journey, you are welcome.

The Devil wants to keep you and your story in darkness. Do not allow that. Revelation 12:11 reminds us, "And they overcame him by the blood of the Lamb, and by the word of their testimony" (KJV).

I understand that you may feel your story is too painful, too small, or that there is no story to tell. But even if you do not have a story yet, I encourage you to begin creating one by faith.

"Now faith is the substance of things hoped for, the evidence of things not seen" (Hebrews 11:1 KJV).

Your postpartum journey matters, and your voice is important. As you reflect, I invite you to write your story in your own time and space. Be led by the Holy Spirit as you write honestly, gently, and without pressure. This is your journey. If you feel led and would like to share your story or reflections, you are welcome to email them to <u>overcomepostpartum@gmail.com</u>.

With your permission, selected stories may be shared anonymously on social media to inspire and encourage other women walking through a similar season. Your identity will always remain private.

You are also invited to join our private Facebook community, Overcome Postpartum with Jesus, a safe and supportive space for encouragement, faith, healing, and connection with women who understand this season.

Be sure to also read the Overcome Guide and the Overcome Journal. I recommend reading the book, guide, and journal together, as I believe freedom often begins by letting it out. I would love to hear how they have shaped you or helped you overcome. I welcome it all and pray that God gives you the courage and direction to share.

From God to my heart to yours, with love!

Michael & Florence Chukwu

About the Authors

Florence and Michael Chukwu have known each other since 2016 and have been joyfully married for four years at the time of this writing. Both serve at Impact Christian Center, Washington. Together, they are the proud parents of a beautiful two-year-old daughter who brings love, joy, and inspiration into their lives. As a family, they love Jesus Christ as their Lord and Savior and are committed to serving God, fulfilling His will, and bringing light into darkness. As entrepreneurs and co-laborers in Christ, their mission is to honor God in all they do and impact lives for His kingdom.

Michael Chukwu works in corporate America and is also a career coach. He is the founder of Raise Careers, where he helps individuals navigate the job market, grow professionally, and achieve career success through modern, strategically designed career tools and coaching.

Florence is an entrepreneur and the founder of SeekFirstHisKingdom.com, a Christian blog where she shares faith-filled teachings, reflections, and encouragement for believers seeking a closer walk with God. She is also the co-founder of Raise Careers, a platform dedicated to empowering professionals through AI-enhanced career development tools, coaching, and education.

Though not writers by profession, Michael and Florence Chukwu write with passion, obedience, and humility. Every page of their work is inspired by the Holy Spirit. Florence sees herself simply as a willing vessel, someone who loves God deeply and strives to do the things that bring Him glory.

To learn more and access additional resources, visit:

https://establishwithgrace.com